Choose
PRAYER

3-MINUTE DEVOTIONS
for Teen Girls

Print ISBN 978-1-63609-960-6

Published by Barbour Publishing, Inc., 1810 Barbour Drive, Uhrichsville, Ohio 44683, www.barbourbooks.com

Our mission is to inspire the world with the life-changing message of the Bible.

Member of the
Evangelical Christian
Publishers Association

Printed in China.

HILARY BERNSTEIN

Choose
PRAYER

3-MINUTE DEVOTIONS
for Teen Girls

BARBOUR
PUBLISHING

INTRODUCTION

Have you ever felt like you *should* pray but don't know what to do? What is prayer, anyway? Do you need to use any special words?

Prayer is a conversation between you and God. This book was written not only to help you understand *how* to pray but also to encourage you *why* to choose prayer. To learn and practice how to pray, you'll only need to spend about three minutes with each devotion.

First, read God's Word. It's filled with examples of actual prayers people prayed. Listen to what other people sound like when they pray. What's their attitude when they come to the Lord? What kind of words do they choose?

Next, read through a short devotion that can help you understand the scripture better and apply the Bible to your own life.

Finally, take time to pray on your own. Practice what you've learned!

These devotions aren't meant to replace your personal time in the Word. Instead, use them to jump-start your habit of spending time with God every day. Learn how and why to come to Him in prayer.

As you read these devotions, take some time to learn how to pray. . .and choose prayer!

CALLING ON HIS NAME

To Seth also a son was born; and he named him Enosh.
Then people began to call upon the name of the Lord.

GENESIS 4:26 NASB

Adam and Eve were the first man and woman to be created by God. Genesis explains that in the Garden of Eden, Adam and Eve walked with God and talked with God, and it was very good.

Once they sinned, though, their perfect conversations with the Lord were forever changed. And once Adam and Eve had children, their sons didn't obey the Lord. In fact, Cain killed his brother, Abel.

Adam and Eve's grandson, Enosh, would've heard about his grandparents' relationship with God in the Garden. When Enosh was alive, people began to call upon the name of the Lord. That means they prayed.

Just like these early people felt compelled to approach the Lord, you can call upon His name too. As you seek Him, call on His name!

LORD, I AM SO GRATEFUL I CAN CALL ON YOU!
THANK YOU THAT YOU WELCOME ME TO APPROACH YOU.

SHOW ME WHAT I SHOULD DO

Tell me in the morning about your love, because I trust you.
Show me what I should do, because my prayers go up to you.
PSALM 143:8 NCV

Life is confusing! No matter how old you get, you'll always be faced with some decisions that leave you feeling confused.

The amazing comfort is that you don't have to worry about figuring everything out on your own, because you can ask your heavenly Father! He's the giver of all good gifts, including wisdom. Wisdom is necessary when the choice you need to make doesn't seem so simple.

Instead of expecting God to make your decision clear right away, ask Him to show you what you should do. Then pay careful attention to the situations in your life and the truth you might hear over and over in different ways. As you listen for God to answer your prayers, He'll show you what you should do.

FATHER, I DO TRUST YOU.
PLEASE SHOW ME WHAT I SHOULD DO!

HE IS WITH YOU

The word of the Lord came to me, saying, "Before I formed you in the womb I knew you, before you were born I set you apart.... "Alas, Sovereign Lord," I said, "I do not know how to speak; I am too young." But the Lord said to me, "Do not say, 'I am too young.' You must go to everyone I send you to and say whatever I command you. Do not be afraid of them, for I am with you and will rescue you."

JEREMIAH 1:4–8 NIV

Before you existed, the Lord knew you. He formed you just the way you are and planned your life. When you feel nervous about the things He asks you to do, tell Him about your hesitation. Admit when you're afraid. Instead of feeling stuck in your fear, ask Him to help. Ask for His strength. Ask Him to work through you. You don't have to be afraid, because He's with you. He will rescue you.

LORD, I'M SO GLAD YOU'RE WITH ME. I WANT TO
TRUST YOU AND NOT LIVE IN FEAR.

I NEED HELP!

*Help me, L<small>ORD</small> my God; save me according
to your unfailing love.*
P<small>SALM</small> 109:26 <small>NIV</small>

Many people don't like asking for help. If you can figure out a way to make something happen or do it all by yourself, it can feel very satisfying to do the work all on your own.

Yet you were not created to live all alone. You're not expected to do absolutely everything all by yourself. God created you to be part of a bigger community—that's a very good reason He created families. Aside from the family and friends in your own life who would love to help you, you're never alone. God is there! When you know you can't do things all by yourself, ask Him for His help.

When you ask for His help, know that no request is too big for Him. His love never fails and it never ends. He will help you and save you.

LORD MY GOD. PLEASE HELP ME! I KNOW YOUR
LOVE NEVER ENDS. PLEASE SAVE ME!

SPEAKING WITHOUT FEAR

"And now, Lord, listen to their threats.
Lord, help us, your servants, to speak your
word without fear. Show us your power to
heal. Give proofs and make miracles happen
by the power of Jesus, your holy servant."
ACTS 4:29–30 NCV

After Jesus died, rose from the dead, and went to heaven, His disciples faced a lot of trouble from Jewish leaders. In fact, many nonbelievers threatened members of the early church. Peter, John, and their friends didn't know what to do about the threats. But they knew they needed to tell everyone about Jesus. When they faced danger and opposition, the best thing the disciples did was pray for God to step in and work. They asked for God's help and power.

Just like the early disciples, when you face danger and opposition, pray! Ask God for His help. Ask Him to keep you from being afraid. And ask Him to make miracles happen. You don't have to face your troubles alone!

LORD, PLEASE HELP ME! I WANT TO SPEAK YOUR WORD WITHOUT FEAR. MAKE MIRACLES HAPPEN AND HELP ME DO IT.

PROTECTED

Do not withhold your mercy from me, LORD;
may your love and faithfulness always protect me.
PSALM 40:11 NIV

When you face difficulties and tough situations in life, sometimes you might feel like it's more than you can handle. Enough is enough. You just want all your challenges and trials to stop!

Cry out to the Lord for His mercy. Honestly tell Him that you can't carry this heavy weight anymore. You need His faithful love and compassion. You need His help!

After you've begged for His mercy, ask for His protection too. Not only can He protect you physically, but He'll also protect you mentally, emotionally, and spiritually. All of this protection is just a part of His love and His faithfulness.

LORD, IT'S SUCH A RELIEF TO KNOW THAT YOUR LOVE
AND FAITHFULNESS WILL ALWAYS KEEP ME SAFE!
THANK YOU FOR YOUR MERCY AND PROTECTION!

SADNESS

*When I heard these things, I sat down and cried for several
days. I was sad and fasted. I prayed to the God of heaven,
"Lord, God of heaven, you are the great God who is to be
respected. You are loyal, and you keep your agreement
with those who love you and obey your commands."*
NEHEMIAH 1:4–5 NCV

Unfortunately, bad news is part of life. You might hear something that breaks your heart or disappoints you. When you do hear bad news, it's okay to be sad about it. Cry. Don't feel like you need to be cheery or pretend like everything is all right. Spend some time in your grief and mourn.

Yet don't forget to include the Lord in your emotional response. Remember who He is and pray, even as your heart feels like it's breaking. Praise the Lord even in your sadness. Remember He is great. He is loyal. He should be respected. He keeps His promises to all who love and obey Him.

LORD GOD OF HEAVEN, YOU ARE THE GREAT AND
LOYAL GOD. I RESPECT, LOVE, AND OBEY YOU.

FORGIVEN

For the sake of your name, Lᴏʀᴅ, forgive my many sins.
Psᴀʟᴍ 25:11 ɴᴄᴠ

Whether you call it messing up, making a mistake, doing what you know you shouldn't do, or sinning, you do wrong things every single day. Absolutely every person does. It's impossible to live a sinless, perfect life of innocence.

Even though everyone sins, it's not like you should celebrate your sin. And it's not like you're invited to keep sinning more because you feel like you can't help yourself.

When you know you've done something wrong, stop and apologize. First, apologize to the Lord, then apologize to anyone you've wronged. After you've apologized, ask for forgiveness. Once you ask God for forgiveness, it's time to change your ways. If you know you keep repeating the same sins over and over again, ask Him for help to change. Ask Him to help take your temptation away.

LORD, I'M SORRY THAT I'VE SINNED AGAINST YOU.
PLEASE FORGIVE ME! PLEASE HELP ME MOVE PAST MY
SINS AND STOP GIVING IN TO TEMPTATION.

DEALING WITH DOUBT

*But Moses said to God, "I am not a great man! How can
I go to the king and lead the Israelites out of Egypt?"*
EXODUS 3:11 NCV

When you read the story of Moses in Exodus, you'll discover
that God asked him to do some pretty amazing, very gutsy,
and ridiculously brave things. At first, Moses wasn't so sure,
and he told God about his doubts and fears. But the Lord
had other plans and proved time after time that He could
use Moses in mighty ways.

God may have amazing plans for you and your life
too. He can use you in mighty ways. When you feel like He's
pushing you to do something that seems scary, tell Him
your doubts and fears. Don't be afraid to admit that you're
wondering why He's choosing you. You don't have to hide
your feelings from the Lord.

LORD, YOU HAVE SO MANY TRULY WONDERFUL THINGS PLANNED
FOR THOSE WHO LOVE YOU. I LOVE YOU! AND I'M WILLING TO
DO WHAT YOU'VE PLANNED FOR ME, EVEN IF IT'S SCARY.

KNOWN

Lord, you have examined me and know all about me.
You know when I sit down and when I get up. You know
my thoughts before I think them. You know where I
go and where I lie down. You know everything I do.
Lord, even before I say a word, you already know it.
PSALM 139:1–4 NCV

When you feel misunderstood or unknown, misheard or unseen, stop yourself. No matter how people make you feel, it's time to examine what is true.

The truth is that the Lord knows everything about you. He understands you. He knows you absolutely and completely. He knows when you get up and when you sit down. He knows when you sleep and when you wake. He knows what you're thinking, He knows what you'll say, and He knows what you've already said. He hears every single prayer you pray. He sees you, He hears you, He knows you. . . and He loves you.

LORD, IT'S AMAZING TO REALIZE THAT YOU KNOW ABSOLUTELY
EVERYTHING ABOUT ME AND CHOOSE TO LOVE ME.

PEACE BE WITH YOU ALL

The God who gives peace be with you all. Amen.
ROMANS 15:33 NCV

When you pray, it can be easy to focus on your own concerns. After all, you know what you're facing. You know how you feel. You know what you want to talk with God about.

Yet it's important to pray for other people too. Pray for those you love. Pray for your family members and friends. Pray for people you don't know very well. Pray for people you don't know at all.

When you pray for others, don't limit yourself to only asking certain requests they may have asked you. Pray bigger prayers. Pray that God would fill their lives with His peace. Pray that God would be with them and guide them. Pray the Lord would work in their lives in amazing ways.

As you pray these bold prayers, know you're trusting in the Lord to do good not only in your own life but also in the lives of others.

FATHER, I PRAISE YOU FOR BEING THE GOD WHO GIVES
PEACE. HELP ME SEE WHO I NEED TO PRAY FOR TODAY.

SEARCHING

God, you are my God. I search for you. I thirst for you like someone in a dry, empty land where there is no water. I have seen you in the Temple and have seen your strength and glory. Because your love is better than life, I will praise you. I will praise you as long as I live.

Psalm 63:1–4 NCV

Each day, it may feel like you need to search for God. Circumstances may seem less than ideal, and you have to really look to find God in the moment. When you find Him, you'll notice He hasn't changed. He's still the God who has infinite strength and glory. He's still the God who loves you with a love that's even better than life.

This God is right there waiting for you. Praise Him for all the amazing and wonderful things you appreciate about Him. Lift up your hands and praise Him because He is a God who can be found.

GOD, YOU ARE MY GOD. I AM SO GLAD THAT
WHEN I SEARCH FOR YOU, I CAN FIND YOU.

SINKING DEEP

While Jonah was inside the fish, he prayed to the Lord
his God and said, "When I was in danger, I called to
the Lord, and he answered me. I was about to die,
so I cried to you, and you heard my voice. You threw
me into the sea, down, down into the deep sea."
JONAH 2:1–3 NCV

God had a specific mission for Jonah to accomplish, yet Jonah ran away to avoid obeying God. His attempt to flee only ended in disaster: he was thrown off a ship in a storm and sank before being swallowed by a big fish. Even with all that adventure, Jonah didn't die. Instead, he prayed while he was sinking and near death, and he prayed while spending three days inside the fish.

While you may never end up in a fish, you'll disobey or even try to run from God at some point. Once you realize you should follow and obey the Lord, pray! Pray when it feels like you're sinking deep. Pray when you need a second chance. Pray when it feels like you're drowning.

FATHER, SOME DAYS IT FEELS LIKE I'M
SINKING IN LIFE. PLEASE HELP ME!

LIFE WITHOUT FEAR

*Even if I walk through a very dark valley, I will
not be afraid, because you are with me. Your
rod and your shepherd's staff comfort me.*

PSALM 23:4 NCV

The Lord is your shepherd. He willingly and lovingly guides you through all the good and all the bad parts of life. The comforting thing is that He'll never leave you. Even when it seems like your life's path is rocky or unstable, He's there. He's with you. You don't have to be afraid.

When fear comes rushing in, threatening to take over your thoughts, tell your Father. Talk with Him about what seems to threaten your peace of mind. You can honestly tell Him how you feel, knowing He's there to gently comfort you.

LORD, KNOWING YOU ARE MY SHEPHERD IS A HUGE RELIEF.
I DON'T NEED TO TRY TO FIGURE THINGS OUT ON MY
OWN. NO MATTER HOW ALONE I FEEL, YOU ARE WITH ME.
I CHOOSE NOT TO LIVE IN FEAR, BECAUSE YOU ARE GOD.

NO STUMBLING

To him who is able to keep you from stumbling and to present you before his glorious presence without fault and with great joy—to the only God our Savior be glory, majesty, power and authority, through Jesus Christ our Lord, before all ages, now and forevermore! Amen.

JUDE 1:24–25 NIV

Sometimes it feels like you're stumbling, bumbling, and mumbling through life. As much as you try to do what's right, you stumble into sin. When it comes time to make a decision, you don't know what you should do, so you bumble around with uncertainty. And some days you mumble the wrong thing or have no idea what to say.

Good news! You don't have to sweat all your missteps. God loves you, and He's able to keep you from stumbling. At the end of your life, because of your faith in Jesus Christ, you'll be in His glorious presence without fault and with great joy. When you pray, remind yourself of these truths, and thank God for each one.

LORD, IT'S ABSOLUTELY AMAZING TO KNOW YOU WORK IN MY HEART AND MY LIFE. THANK YOU FOR KEEPING ME FROM STUMBLING! I PRAISE YOU!

CREATED TO UNDERSTAND

You made me and formed me with your hands.
Give me understanding so I can learn your commands.
PSALM 119:73 NCV

The Lord Almighty created you with great care, love, and intention. He made you just the way you are. With His own hands He formed you.

Sometimes His commands can seem confusing. You may not be sure you want to follow them. But instead of ignoring or forgetting His commands, ask the Lord to help you understand what He's asked you to do. Pray that He would help you learn His commands. When you ask for wisdom to better understand Him, He'll give it.

LORD, I'M IN AWE OF YOU. THANK YOU FOR CREATING ME JUST THE WAY I AM. I HAVE A HARD TIME UNDERSTANDING EVERYTHING YOU'D LIKE ME TO DO. WOULD YOU PLEASE HELP ME? PLEASE SHOW ME HOW I CAN BETTER UNDERSTAND YOU.

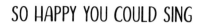

SO HAPPY YOU COULD SING

David sang this song to the LORD when the LORD saved him
from Saul and all his other enemies. He said: "The LORD is my
rock, my fortress, my Savior. My God is my rock. I can run to
him for safety. He is my shield and my saving strength, my
defender and my place of safety. . . . I will call to the LORD, who
is worthy of praise, and I will be saved from my enemies."
2 SAMUEL 22:1–4 NCV

Think about a time when you couldn't help but sing. There's something about music that you just can't keep inside. The same can be said about happiness or joy—you can't keep all the good feelings to yourself.

Just like David sang when he had a huge victory, you can sing to the Lord. When you know God has answered your prayers, thank Him! Praise the Lord when you're happy! Sing to Him when He brings relief. Create a song that reminds you of all the wonderful things He's done.

LORD, YOU'RE MY ROCK AND FORTRESS. I CAN RUN TO YOU
FOR SAFETY. YOU'RE MY STRENGTH AND SHIELD. YOU'RE MY
DEFENDER AND MY SAFE PLACE. YOU'RE WORTHY OF MY PRAISE!

LEADING AND GUIDING

*Send me your light and truth to guide me. Let them
lead me to your holy mountain, to where you live.*

PSALM 43:3 NCV

Life can be confusing. Some days it might feel like you're in
the dark and have no idea which way to turn. Other days you
realize you need to make a decision from so many different
choices, and you have no clue what's best.

When you have no idea what to do or decide, don't try
to figure things out on your own. Don't even talk over all
your options again and again with your best friend. Stop
yourself and pray. Ask God to guide you. Ask Him to lead you
and make your way clear. He'll send His light and His truth
to guide you. He'll lead you, but you need to ask Him first.

FATHER, HELP ME REMEMBER TO ASK YOU FIRST! WHEN I'M
CONFUSED, PLEASE GUIDE ME. WHEN I DON'T KNOW WHAT
CHOICE TO MAKE, PLEASE LEAD ME TO THE RIGHT DECISION.

SEEN

She gave this name to the Lord who spoke to
her: "You are the God who sees me," for she said,
"I have now seen the One who sees me."
GENESIS 16:13 NIV

In Genesis, we can read about the story of Hagar, a pregnant woman who was running away from her problems. Nothing in her life seemed ideal. And as she found herself alone, she debated what she would do next. The angel of the Lord came and talked with Hagar, filling her with encouragement and hope. When their conversation was over, Hagar knew that God saw her.

He was the God who saw Hagar, and He is the God who sees you.

When you feel alone or find yourself in a situation you never imagined, remember God is the God who sees you. He sees you, He hears you, He knows you, and He loves you.

FATHER, YOU ARE THE GOD WHO SEES ME.
THANK YOU THAT I'M NEVER ALONE!

EXAMINATION TIME

Examine me, Lord, and put me to the test; refine my mind and my heart. For Your goodness is before my eyes, and I have walked in Your truth.

PSALM 26:2–3 NASB

It can be so easy to think that no one sees what you're doing or no one knows what you're thinking. So when the psalmist asks God to examine him and put him to the test, it can seem scary. Ask God to examine me? Put me to the test?

The thing is, God already knows. When He examines you, don't think about the ways He sees all you're doing wrong. Don't worry if He notices all the things you "should" be doing. Instead, ask Him to examine you so that your mind and your heart can improve. Asking God to change you will only make you better. Put His goodness before you in what you see and say and do, and you won't have to worry about any examination.

LORD. YOU KNOW ME. YOU KNOW MY HEART AND MY MIND. EXAMINE ME SO I CAN WALK IN YOUR TRUTH.

DEALING WITH GUILT AND SHAME

I prayed, "My God, I am too ashamed and embarrassed to lift up my face to you, my God, because our sins are so many. They are higher than our heads. Our guilt even reaches up to the sky."
EZRA 9:6 NCV

No matter how good of a life you think you're living, when you realize how holy and perfect God is, your own imperfections are magnified. It can feel embarrassing to come to the Lord in prayer when you feel the shame or disgust of your sin.

In the Bible, Ezra and the Israelites dealt with guilt and shame. Their sins, too many to count, weighed heavily on their consciences. But Ezra came to the Lord in prayer anyway. He asked for forgiveness, and the Israelites turned away from their sins to pursue the Lord.

You can do the same! When you realize your sins, pray for forgiveness. Ask the Lord to help you turn around and stop sinning.

GOD, I AM TOO ASHAMED AND EMBARRASSED BECAUSE
MY SINS ARE SO MANY. PLEASE FORGIVE ME! PLEASE
HELP ME LIVE A LIFE THAT PLEASES YOU.

HELP!

Lord, my Rock, I call out to you for help.
Do not be deaf to me. If you are silent, I will
be like those in the grave. Hear the sound of
my prayer, when I cry out to you for help.
PSALM 28:1–2 NCV

Just like you'd ask for help whenever you feel stuck in a situation, call out to God for help too. Simply pray without speaking a word. Communicate with the Lord through your thoughts. And as your mind is racing and you know you need help or understanding or guidance, ask Him. Call out to Him for help, either by saying the words out loud or to yourself.

When you do call out to Him for help, you might feel like you're waiting endlessly for Him to respond. Know that He does hear you, and even if you don't see immediate results, He is answering your prayer in His own way.

LORD, MY ROCK, HELP! PLEASE LISTEN TO
MY PRAYER. I NEED YOUR HELP!

HOLY, HOLY, HOLY

*Each of the four living creatures had six
wings and was covered with eyes all around,
even under its wings. Day and night they never
stop saying: "'Holy, holy, holy is the Lord God
Almighty,' who was, and is, and is to come."*

REVELATION 4:8 NIV

Heaven contains sights and sounds and experiences we can never fully imagine in this earthly life. When writers of the Bible try to describe certain scenes, it's hard to comprehend. Living creatures with six wings and a bunch of eyes? It sounds like something that belongs in a science fiction movie.

Besides the unusual description of the creatures, notice what they spend all their time saying: "'Holy, holy, holy is the Lord God Almighty,' who was, and is, and is to come."

Just like that's being proclaimed in heaven, you also can declare it right now in your prayers. When you pray to God, remember that He is holy, meaning blameless, pure, and set apart. Remember He's always been holy. He is holy right at this moment. And He is holy for all of eternity to come.

HOLY, HOLY, HOLY ARE YOU, LORD GOD ALMIGHTY!

THE AGONY OF ENEMIES

Lord, I have many enemies! Many people have
turned against me. Many are saying about me,
"God won't rescue him." But, Lord, you are my shield,
my wonderful God who gives me courage.
PSALM 3:1–3 NCV

It's no fun to know you have enemies, whether they're frenemies you pretend to get along with or outright enemies who make your life miserable. When people turn against you, it leaves you feeling awful.

If and when you're dealing with frustration, hurt, and anger that come along with enemies, don't try to figure things out on your own. As tempting as it is to dwell on your negative thoughts and feelings, turn things over to the Lord. Ask Him for help, along with some comfort and strength. Pray that He will protect you and give you courage to deal with the situation. Ask Him to rescue you. Trust that He will work all things out for good.

LORD, YOU ARE MY SHIELD. PLEASE PROTECT ME AS I DEAL WITH ALL THE HURT THAT COMES WITH HAVING ENEMIES. PLEASE RESCUE ME FROM THIS SITUATION! PROTECT ME AND GIVE ME COURAGE.

NOTHING IS TOO HARD

"I prayed to the LORD, Oh, Lord GOD, you made the skies and the earth with your very great power. There is nothing too hard for you to do."
JEREMIAH 32:16–17 NCV

How easy is it to focus on difficulties and what seems to be impossible? While you can get trapped in a thought pattern of focusing on the negative, it's important to learn from Jeremiah's prayer. There is nothing too hard for God to do. Nothing!

When you consider all the Lord has made, from the skies to the earth to all living creatures, He is the God who makes the impossible possible. This great God is worthy of your worship!

As you find yourself facing what seems to be an impossible situation, remind yourself that nothing is too hard for God to do. Then praise and pray to the God of the impossible.

LORD GOD, NOTHING IS TOO HARD FOR YOU TO DO! I PRAISE YOU FOR YOUR MIGHTY POWER AND THE WAY YOU DO THE IMPOSSIBLE.

CONFESS IT

*I acknowledged my sin to You, and I did not hide
my guilt; I said, "I will confess my wrongdoings to
the LORD"; and You forgave the guilt of my sin.*

PSALM 32:5 NASB

Admitting that you're wrong takes a lot of courage. It's humbling to acknowledge that you've made a mistake, whether intentionally or unintentionally. It's embarrassing to own up to your sin.

As much as King David was a man after God's heart, he also sinned. He discovered that when he tried to hide his sin, it only made him feel terrible. Confessing brought freedom.

When you do sin and confess it to the Lord, you'll find freedom. When you stop hiding your guilt and own up to what you've done wrong, He'll forgive you. Come to the Lord with your honest prayers and confession and experience His forgiveness and love.

LORD, I HAVE SINNED AGAINST YOU. I'M SORRY!
I DON'T WANT TO HIDE MY GUILT AND
WRONGDOING ANYMORE. PLEASE FORGIVE ME.

A FRIENDSHIP WITH GOD

The LORD spoke to Moses face to face as a man speaks with his friend. . . . Moses said to the LORD, . . . "You have said to me, 'I know you very well, and I am pleased with you.' If I have truly pleased you, show me your plans so that I may know you and continue to please you."

EXODUS 33:11–13 NCV

From his birth to his death, Moses led an extraordinary life. One amazing fact is that the Lord spoke to Moses face-to-face, just like friends. Part of their friendship involved absolute honesty. Moses shared exactly what he felt and thought with the Lord. He didn't sugarcoat awkward situations or challenges he faced.

Like Moses, you can come to the Lord just like you would come to your friend. Tell Him everything that's on your mind. Your prayers can include all your thoughts and feelings, your happy moments and your fears. Be honest with the Lord and watch how your relationship with Him will grow.

LORD, I WANT TO BE YOUR FRIEND!
I WANT TO BE HONEST WITH YOU.

33

YOU DON'T HAVE TO FIGHT ALONE

Lord, battle with those who battle with me.
Fight against those who fight against me.

PSALM 35:1 NCV

When you face conflict in your life, whether it's a battle of wills or a battle of words, things can get intense. The fantastic news is you don't have to feel like you're facing all the conflict on your own. The Lord is on your side!

Examine your own heart and your motives when you're in the middle of a conflict. Ask God if there's any wrong in your life. If you know there is, confess it and ask for forgiveness, both from the Lord and the person you've offended.

When you feel like it's you against the world and you don't know what to do, ask the Lord for help. Ask Him to fight for you. You don't have to go through life all by yourself.

LORD, PLEASE FIGHT AGAINST THOSE PEOPLE WHO
ARE FIGHTING AGAINST ME. I NEED YOU!

SO MANY POSSIBILITIES

*Lord, heal me, and I will truly be healed. Save me,
and I will truly be saved. You are the one I praise.*
JEREMIAH 17:14 NCV

In today's world of skepticism, it can be easy to doubt. Can God do all He says He can do? Can the Lord do what seems impossible? Can He heal? Can He save?

The amazing, fantastic reality is that—yes!—God can do all He says He can do. The Lord can do what seems impossible. Through Jesus Christ, God saves. Romans 10:9 (NCV) says, "If you declare with your mouth, 'Jesus is Lord,' and if you believe in your heart that God raised Jesus from the dead, you will be saved."

Not only can God save you, but He also has the power to heal and work many other miracles. A God so full of possibilities deserves your highest praise!

LORD, YOU ARE THE GOD WHO SAVES. YOU ARE THE
GOD WHO HEALS. I PRAISE YOU AND YOU ALONE!

SO DEEP, SO HIGH

*Lord, your love reaches to the heavens, your loyalty to
the skies. Your goodness is as high as the mountains.
Your justice is as deep as the great ocean.*
PSALM 36:5–6 NCV

No matter where you are right now, take a look outside
and find some part of creation that amazes you. Is it how
high the sky is? Is it the moon and the stars at night? Do you
admire the leaves on trees or a stunning sunset?

God made all of those parts of creation. And just like
they're so immense and more detailed than you'll ever
realize, they also do a fantastic job of showing God's love
for you. He loves you so much it's like His love reaches to
the heavens. His loyalty and faithfulness stretch to the sky.
His goodness is as powerful and as tall as mountains. And
His justice is deep like the ocean depths. Soak in all of that
love and loyalty and goodness and justice, and praise Him!

LORD, I PRAISE YOU! THERE IS NO ONE AND NOT A THING
LIKE YOU. YOUR POWER, MIGHT, AND LOVE ASTONISH ME.

WONDERFUL THINGS

LORD, you have done this wonderful thing for
my sake and because you wanted to. You have
made known all these great things.
1 CHRONICLES 17:19 NCV

Throughout King David's life, God led and protected him. David went from shepherding sheep to shepherding the Israelites as their king. All through his life, the Lord blessed him and also promised great blessings to David's descendants. David responded by praising God and acknowledging all the wonderful things He had done.

Like David, when you see the Lord working in your life and you recognize the ways He blesses you, praise Him! Acknowledge that God is the one who does wonderful things for your sake. It's nothing you've done on your own. Rather, it's because God has wanted to bless you in this way.

LORD, YOU HAVE DONE SO MANY WONDERFUL THINGS FOR MY
SAKE SIMPLY BECAUSE YOU WANTED TO. THANK YOU! I PRAISE
YOU FOR YOUR GREATNESS AND WONDERFUL GENEROSITY.

SHARING IT ALL

All my longings lie open before you, Lord;
my sighing is not hidden from you. My heart pounds,
my strength fails me; even the light has gone from
my eyes. My friends and companions avoid me
because of my wounds; my neighbors stay far away.
PSALM 38:9–11 NIV

It can be tempting to keep your feelings to yourself. While it can be very wise to not share all your thoughts and feelings with everyone, it's a really great choice to share your hopes, dreams, thoughts, and ideas with the Lord. After all, He knows you completely. He knows your longings. He knows your frustrations and disappointments. He knows when you're sad and when you're tired. He knows when it feels like you've lost all the pep in your step.

Even if and when other people avoid you, the Lord won't turn away. Rather, the Lord will draw near. All you need is to draw near to Him.

LORD, YOU KNOW ALL I WANT AND ALL I NEED. YOU
KNOW WHAT HAPPENS ON MY WORST DAYS AND ON MY
BEST DAYS. I AM SO GRATEFUL THAT I HAVE YOU.

GUIDANCE AND DIRECTION

*Then he prayed, "L*ORD*, God of my master Abraham, make
me successful today, and show kindness to my master
Abraham. See, I am standing beside this spring, and the
daughters of the townspeople are coming out to draw
water. May it be that when I say to a young woman,
'Please let down your jar that I may have a drink,' and she
says, 'Drink, and I'll water your camels too'—let her be the
one you have chosen for your servant Isaac. By this I will
know that you have shown kindness to my master."*

GENESIS 24:12–14 NIV

In Genesis, Abraham's servant was on a huge mission: finding a wife for Abraham's son Isaac. Instead of just randomly
choosing any woman, though, the servant prayed to God
for guidance and direction.

Like Abraham's servant, ask God to help you when
you're confused. When you have a big decision to make or
a task to begin, pray for the Lord's help. Ask Him for success.
He'll bring clarity in amazing ways.

LORD GOD, PLEASE MAKE IT ABUNDANTLY OBVIOUS
WHAT I SHOULD DO. PLEASE GRANT ME SUCCESS!

SEEING HIS KIND FAITHFULNESS

Then the man bowed down and worshiped the
*L*ORD*, saying, "Praise be to the L*ORD*, the God of*
my master Abraham, who has not abandoned
his kindness and faithfulness to my master."
GENESIS 24:26–27 NIV

When Abraham's servant asked God for guidance and success, the Lord worked in amazing ways. Prayers were answered almost immediately, and the unbelievable became believable. The Lord led Abraham's servant to the absolute perfect wife for Abraham's son Isaac.

After Abraham's servant saw the Lord at work, he didn't shrug it off. He bowed down and worshipped the Lord. He praised God because he recognized the Lord's kindness and faithfulness.

When you know the Lord has answered your prayer and has been kind and faithful to you, worship Him! Praise His holy name and thank Him for His faithful kindness.

PRAISE BE TO YOU, LORD! THANK YOU FOR YOUR KINDNESS AND
FAITHFULNESS TO ME. I CHOOSE TO WORSHIP YOU AND YOU ALONE.

ARE YOU THERE?

How long, Lord, must I call for help, but you do not listen?
Or cry out to you, "Violence!" but you do not save?

HABAKKUK 1:2 NIV

It doesn't always feel like God hears your prayers. If you don't notice an answer to your prayers, you may wonder if He's listening at all.

God hears you. He listens to you. And He's answering your prayers. Because God is God and you're not, He hears and listens and answers in different ways than you expect or even understand.

Instead of getting frustrated if He's not doing everything you want Him to do, remember He won't magically fulfill your every desire. Instead of doubting His goodness or His love for you, wait for Him to show you His good purpose. It may take much longer than you might ever expect, but it doesn't mean He's not at work. Keep calling out to Him. Keep trusting He'll keep working in your life.

LORD, WAITING IS SO DIFFICULT! PLEASE HELP ME
WAIT PATIENTLY FOR YOU. IN THE MEANTIME,
PLEASE SHOW ME IN SOME WAY, EITHER LITTLE OR BIG,
THAT YOU HEAR ME AND THAT YOU'RE AT WORK.

THIRSTING FOR GOD

As the deer pants for streams of water, so my soul pants for you, my God. My soul thirsts for God, for the living God. When can I go and meet with God?
PSALM 42:1–2 NIV

Have you ever felt yourself thirst for God? Think about how you feel after a long, hot day outside. Do you feel that same parched feeling but know that only God can quench your thirst?

When you spend your time focusing on things of the world, it's easy to feel depleted. Yet God is the one to quench your thirst. He's the one who will refresh you and your thirsty soul.

Instead of looking for ways you can feel temporarily satisfied with temporary, earthly pursuits, seek the Lord. Meet with Him, either with your Bible or prayer or both, and watch the way He refreshes you.

I THIRST FOR YOU, GOD. I'M TIRED OF ALL THE QUICK FIXES THIS WORLD OFFERS BECAUSE THEY'RE SO FLEETING. PLEASE SATISFY MY THIRST FOR YOU!

SAFETY AND UNITY

"I am coming to you; I will not stay in the world any longer.
But they are still in the world. Holy Father, keep them
safe by the power of your name, the name you gave me,
so that they will be one, just as you and I are one."
JOHN 17:11 NCV

When Jesus knew His death was nearing, He prayed for His disciples and for followers who would come in future years. In other words, He was praying for you!

How did Jesus pray for you? He prayed you'd be kept safe in this world by the power of God's holy name. He also prayed for unity of believers.

To echo Jesus' prayer, don't be afraid to ask God to keep you safe. When you find yourself disagreeing with another Christ follower, pray about your disagreement. Ask God to help unite you together as the body of Christ.

HOLY FATHER, WHAT A GIFT THAT JESUS PRAYED FOR ME!
LIKE HE PRAYED, PLEASE KEEP ME SAFE BY THE POWER OF YOUR
NAME. PLEASE HELP ME BE UNITED WITH OTHER BELIEVERS SO
THAT WE MAY BE ONE JUST LIKE YOU AND JESUS ARE ONE.

MERCY!

*Answer me when I pray to you, my God who does
what is right. Make things easier for me when I am in
trouble. Have mercy on me and hear my prayer.*

PSALM 4:1 NCV

In the middle of all the troubles of life, God can be trusted as
one who does what is right. Because He is good and because
He hears and answers prayers, it's vital to remember to pray
to Him. Don't try to do things all on your own, whether in
your own power or your own understanding. Ask for His
help! Ask for Him to work and do what is right in your life.
When you feel like life is especially difficult, ask God to make
things easier for you. And when you're facing trouble after
trouble, ask for His mercy.

GOD. YOU ALWAYS DO WHAT IS RIGHT.
PLEASE HELP ME! I PRAY FOR YOUR MERCY
AS I'M IN TROUBLE. PLEASE HEAR MY PRAYERS
AND MAKE THINGS EASIER FOR ME.

HAVE YOU ASKED?

Jabez cried out to the God of Israel, "Oh, that you
would bless me and enlarge my territory! Let your
hand be with me, and keep me from harm so that I will
be free from pain." And God granted his request.

1 CHRONICLES 4:10 NIV

Jabez wasn't shy about asking God for success and blessings.
Boldly he asked the Lord to enlarge his territory and to keep
him from harm. He asked for God's hand to be with him and
to be kept free from pain. And what was God's response?
He granted the request of Jabez.

God is free to answer your request in any way He
chooses, yet Jabez left a great example to not be afraid to
ask for God's favor. Instead of thinking you don't deserve
God's good gifts, ask for His protection and blessing.

FATHER, PLEASE BLESS ME! ENLARGE MY TERRITORY.
LET YOUR HAND BE WITH ME. AND PLEASE, LORD,
KEEP ME FROM HARM SO THAT I WILL BE FREE FROM PAIN.

FRUSTRATED BY WRONG

For you are not a God who is pleased with wickedness;
with you, evil people are not welcome. The arrogant
cannot stand in your presence. You hate all who
do wrong; you destroy those who tell lies. The
bloodthirsty and deceitful you, LORD, detest.
PSALM 5:4–6 NIV

It's hard to live out your faith day after day when you see evil being celebrated in this world. But in Psalm 5, David shows that it's good to come to the Lord even when you're surrounded by bad.

When wickedness, evil, arrogance, lying, and wrong living upset you, tell the Lord about it! In prayer, tell Him what you see wrong with the world. He's not pleased with all the sin either. Yet He can and will do something about it. He detests what's wrong and will destroy evil.

Instead of bottling up all your frustration, anger, and disgust, tell God about it. Ask for Him to work. Ask for His help in navigating life right now. He'll hear your prayer and respond.

LORD, YOU ARE PERFECT! YOU ARE HOLY. I PRAY YOU WOULD
PUT AN END TO ALL THE WICKEDNESS AND EVIL AROUND ME.

QUESTIONS?

After these things happened, the Lord spoke his word to Abram in a vision: "Abram, don't be afraid. I will defend you, and I will give you a great reward." But Abram said, "Lord God, what can you give me? . . . Look, you have given me no son, so a slave born in my house will inherit everything I have."

GENESIS 15:1–3 NCV

After God told Abram a great promise for his future, Abram didn't celebrate or even thank the Lord. He questioned God. Not understanding how the Lord would fulfill His promise, Abram was caught up in the details. Before accepting God's promise with belief, he wanted answers.

Abram became the father of many nations all through God's faithfulness and miraculous gifts. If Abram questioned God, don't feel embarrassed to ask God for clarification. Ask for understanding if you feel like you need it. The important thing is to come to your heavenly Father with honesty. Work through your questions with Him.

FATHER, PLEASE HELP ME UNDERSTAND YOUR WILL FOR MY LIFE. PLEASE HELP ME TRUST YOU IN FAITH!

BELIEVING BY FAITH

Abram believed the LORD. And the LORD accepted Abram's
faith, and that faith made him right with God.

GENESIS 15:6 NCV

Just because Abram questioned the Lord's ability and plan, it didn't mean that he didn't believe the Lord. Ultimately, through his faith, Abram chose to believe that God could deliver on His great promises. And God did.

Just like Abram is praised for his faith and belief, you can be too. When you feel like you're plagued with doubt, ask God for understanding, then choose to step out in faith and believe. Watch the way God will fulfill His promises and be faithful in your life. Believe the Lord. Your faith will make you right with God.

FATHER GOD, I WANT TO BELIEVE YOU! I WANT TO
STEP OUT IN FAITH AND DO THE UNBELIEVABLE AND
SEEMINGLY IMPOSSIBLE THINGS YOU'VE CALLED ME TO DO.
PLEASE HELP ME AS I WALK STEP-BY-STEP WITH YOU.

DOUBLE-CHECKING

God said to Abram, "I am the LORD who led you
out of Ur of Babylonia so that I could give you
this land to own." But Abram said, "Lord GOD,
how can I be sure that I will own this land?"
GENESIS 15:7–8 NCV

Even after Abram chose to believe the Lord through faith,
he continued to question the Lord's ways. Abram asked the
Lord for certainty.

God has a plan for you and your life. He knows exactly
how He will work all things together for His good purposes.
He will lead you where you need to go for His specific reasons.
Yet He still welcomes your questions. Instead of barging
ahead, thinking you know the exact thing He's planned for
you to do, ask Him. Check along the way, and if you need
certainty, ask Him for that. Keep walking by faith and keep
communicating with your heavenly Father.

THANK YOU, FATHER, FOR THE AMAZING PLANS YOU HAVE FOR
ME. I PRAY YOU'LL MAKE THINGS OBVIOUS FOR ME. SHOW ME THE
WAY I SHOULD GO. HELP ME BOLDLY AND BRAVELY FOLLOW YOU
IN FAITH. I WANT TO LIVE OUT YOUR PURPOSES FOR MY LIFE.

WHO GETS THE GLORY?

Not to us, LORD, not to us but to your name be the
glory, because of your love and faithfulness.
PSALM 115:1 NIV

Someone gets glory for things that are accomplished. In your life, who usually gets the glory? Do you take credit when the spotlight shines on you? Do you give credit to someone else? Or do you choose to give all the glory to God?

When you see the Lord working and acting in your life and in the world, don't be afraid to give God the glory. Give Him praise. Give Him credit. Because of His love and faithfulness, He works in amazing ways. Whether it's through the things you say or the prayers you pray, shine the spotlight on the Lord. Give Him glory and thanks and praise for working in His amazing ways.

FATHER, I GIVE YOU ALL THE GLORY! YOU HAVE
WORKED IN A WONDERFUL WAY BECAUSE OF YOUR
LOVE AND FAITHFULNESS. I PRAISE YOU!

STRENGTH

*Then Samson prayed to the L*ORD*, "Lord G*OD*, remember me. God, please give me strength one more time so I can pay these Philistines back for putting out my two eyes!"*
JUDGES 16:28 NCV

Samson lived a life doing the Lord's purpose until he was distracted and tempted by Delilah. After he chose to follow his own way instead of the Lord's, he suffered greatly. In what would be his final work on this earth, Samson prayed for the Lord's strength so he could punish the Philistines. Samson would sacrifice his own life in this act, and he knew it was a suicide mission. Yet he knew the one who could provide enough strength to accomplish the task. He knew the one who could make the impossible possible.

Hopefully you won't be led astray like Samson. Hopefully you'll choose to live a life of devotion and obedience. But regardless of your life choices and obedience, don't forget you can always pray to the Lord to give you strength. You can always call on Him when you need Him the most.

LORD GOD, PLEASE GIVE ME STRENGTH TO DO YOUR GOOD WORK!

GLORY AND HONOR AND POWER

*"You are worthy, our Lord and God, to receive glory
and honor and power, for you created all things, and
by your will they were created and have their being."*
REVELATION 4:11 NIV

Even if it's easy to forget who you're praying to, remember
that you get the privilege of praying to the God of the universe! Because of who He is, He is worthy of your glory. He's
worthy of Your honor. He's worthy of your praise. He created
every single thing in creation. He has willed for life to exist,
including your life, and He created humans in His own image.
At the very least, He deserves your thanks.

One fantastic way to thank Him is to pray to Him
and praise His name. You can honor Him by praying with
respect and a holy fear. He is God Almighty. He is worthy
of your praise.

LORD GOD, I PRAISE YOU! YOU CREATED ALL THINGS, INCLUDING ME.
YOU ARE COMPLETELY POWERFUL AND SO VERY GOOD. I HONOR YOU.

WOW!

*I look at your heavens, which you made with
your fingers. I see the moon and stars, which you
created. But why are people even important to
you? Why do you take care of human beings?*

PSALM 8:3–4 NCV

Look outside. In fact, if it's possible, get up, go outside,
and look up. What do you see? Whether it's day or night,
look up at the heavens. God made them with His fingers.
He made the moon. He made the stars. He made the sun.
He made the clouds. Everything amazing you see? God
made it all. Consider the beauty of creation, and then
consider that the God who created the heavens and the
earth also created you.

Because of the way He's not only created you but also
cares for you every single day, it's time to thank Him. Praise
Him for the way He cares just for you.

LORD, YOU ARE AMAZING! I CAN'T EVEN IMAGINE HOW YOU'VE
CREATED EVERYTHING, BUT I'M SO GRATEFUL THAT YOU
HAVE—AND THAT YOU CARE FOR EVERYTHING TOO.

THE GOD OF MIRACLES

On the day that the Lord gave up the Amorites to the Israelites, Joshua stood before all the people of Israel and said to the Lord: "Sun, stand still over Gibeon. Moon, stand still over the Valley of Aijalon." So the sun stood still, and the moon stopped until the people defeated their enemies. . . . The sun stopped in the middle of the sky and waited to go down for a full day.

JOSHUA 10:12–13 NCV

God is a God of miracles. And once when the Israelites were in battle, their leader, Joshua, prayed for the sun and moon to stand still until they were victorious. God not only brought a victory for the Israelites, but He also stopped the sun and moon in their places for a full day.

You may never witness a miracle like the sun stopping, but you can remember that the God you pray to is the God of miracles.

LORD GOD, YOU ARE ABSOLUTELY AMAZING!
I'M SO GRATEFUL I CAN COME TO YOU AT ANY TIME.
NO PRAYER REQUEST IS TOO BIG FOR YOU!

HOW TO PRAY

Jesus said to them, "When you pray, say: 'Father, may your name always be kept holy. May your kingdom come. Give us the food we need for each day. Forgive us for our sins, because we forgive everyone who has done wrong to us. And do not cause us to be tempted.'"

LUKE 11:2–4 NCV

During His time on earth, Jesus taught others how to pray, so there's no need for guessing what to say. As Jesus taught, our prayers need to acknowledge God's holiness. He's worthy of our praise. We should ask Him to bring His kingdom here to earth, and for our daily food.

Asking for forgiveness and to forgive others are both important requests to remember. Finally, you can ask for God to help you stand strong against temptation. As you pray like Jesus modeled, you can cover all the necessary areas of your life.

FATHER. MAY YOUR NAME BE KEPT HOLY. MAY YOUR KINGDOM COME. PLEASE GIVE ME FOOD I NEED TODAY. PLEASE FORGIVE MY SINS. HELP ME FORGIVE OTHERS AND PROTECT ME FROM TEMPTATION.

HE KNOWS

*You have recorded my troubles. You have kept a
list of my tears. Aren't they in your records?*
PSALM 56:8 NCV

You're never alone. Even on your worst, most heartbroken
days, the Lord is there. He knows all the troubles you have,
and He pays attention to every single tear you cry. While
sadness is part of this life, you're not alone when you face
hard times. The Lord pays attention to all of your anger, all
of your grief, all of your confusion.

Because God sees and knows, you don't have to spend
time explaining details to Him. He understands. You can
just pour out your feelings and tell Him what you're thinking. Be completely honest and trust that your feelings are
meaningful not just to you but also to your heavenly Father.

FATHER, I WISH I DIDN'T HAVE TO GO THROUGH HARD
TIMES. BUT SINCE I DO, I'M SO GRATEFUL I'M NOT
GOING THROUGH THEM ALONE. I AM RELIEVED THAT
YOU'RE ALWAYS THERE, AND YOU ALWAYS KNOW.

TALKING WITH GOD

Now when Abram was ninety-nine years old, the Lord
appeared to Abram and said to him, "I am God Almighty;
walk before Me, and be blameless. I will make My covenant
between Me and you, and I will multiply you exceedingly."
Abram fell on his face, and God talked with him.
GENESIS 17:1–3 NASB

Abram was an ordinary man who experienced something
extraordinary when he was old. God appeared to him and
talked with him. This was not an everyday occurrence. In
fact, Abram fell on his face when he experienced this.

Out of everyone, God chose Abram. He chose to make
a specific promise with him, and He chose to talk with him.
Even though you're not Abram, you can still follow God's
requests for Abram. You can choose to walk before God.
You can try to be blameless. Yes, everyone sins, but there's
a big difference between willfully choosing to sin and trying
to live a life that's blameless. You also can choose to talk
with God through prayer.

GOD ALMIGHTY, YOU ARE HOLY! I WANT TO WALK
BEFORE YOU AND KNOW YOU MORE!

A WILLINGNESS FOR GOD'S WILL

Then Jesus went away a second time and prayed, "My Father,
if it is not possible for this painful thing to be taken from me,
and if I must do it, I pray that what you want will be done."
MATTHEW 26:42 NCV

Life doesn't always turn out the way you'd hoped. Sometimes you face situations you'd rather completely skip. Jesus understands.

Instead of ignoring His feelings, Jesus honestly prayed. He asked His Father to change the situation and take it away from Him. When you pray, you can follow Jesus' example and honestly talk to God about your feelings.

After He shared how He felt, Jesus made an important decision: "If I must do it, I pray that what you want will be done." That attitude and decision are essential to a life of faith. Ask God for His will to be done, no matter what you might feel.

MY FATHER, IF I MUST DO WHAT I DON'T WANT TO DO,
I PRAY THAT WHAT YOU WANT WILL BE DONE.

ASKING FOR FORGIVENESS

*Lord, don't correct me when you are angry; don't punish
me when you are very angry. Lord, have mercy on me
because I am weak. Heal me, Lord, because my bones
ache. I am very upset. Lord, how long will it be?*
PSALM 6:1–3 NCV

Every single person sins. As much as you might try to intentionally live a perfect life, you'll make mistakes. You'll choose responses that aren't right. Your sin and wrong choices will separate you from God and His perfection.

Even if you feel pulled to make a wrong choice or if you know you've done something to upset the Lord, you can still come to Him. You don't have to hide away in shame. When you know you've done wrong, simply tell Him. Admit your mistake, ask for forgiveness, and be grateful for the Lord's mercy.

LORD, PLEASE FORGIVE ME! I'VE DONE WRONG AND I'M SORRY.
PLEASE DON'T PUNISH ME. INSTEAD, PLEASE HAVE MERCY ON ME!

EVERYDAY BLESSINGS

Say to him, "Save us, God our Savior, and bring us
back and save us from other nations. Then we will
thank you and will gladly praise you." Praise the Lord,
the God of Israel. He always was and always will be.
All the people said "Amen" and praised the Lord.

1 Chronicles 16:35–36 ncv

The Israelites, God's chosen people, were able to think back on all the ways the Lord rescued them throughout their history. When they were conquered by other nations, over and over the Lord saved them and brought them back to their land. Because of His faithful rescue, time and time again, they thanked and praised Him.

Like the Israelites, when you spy God at work in your life, thank Him! Praise Him for the ways He works the miraculous, whether you notice big gifts from Him or tiny ones. Look for Him at work in your day, and every day you'll find evidence of the way He loves and saves you.

GOD MY SAVIOR. I PRAISE YOU! THANK YOU FOR
THE WAY YOU RESCUE ME. YOU ALWAYS WERE AND
ALWAYS WILL BE. I GLADLY PRAISE YOU.

EVERY GOOD THING

Protect me, God, because I trust in you.
I said to the LORD, "You are my Lord.
Every good thing I have comes from you."
PSALM 16:1–2 NCV

How would your life be different if you realized that every good thing you have comes from God?

Instead of thinking you deserve blessings or work hard enough to make good things happen, your life and your prayers will change when you begin to realize that all the good that happens to you comes from the Lord.

God will protect you. Not only is He a protective Father, but He also is trustworthy. He knows when you trust Him, and He loves to lavish you with good gifts. Take just a moment to think about every good thing in your life. You might think of things that happened today or things that happened years ago. Think about the good and thank God for each of these good, good gifts.

LORD, I DO TRUST YOU. YOU ARE MY LORD!
THANK YOU SO MUCH FOR EVERY GOOD THING I HAVE.
THEY ARE GOOD, GOOD GIFTS FROM YOU.

WHY?

*Moses returned to the Lord and said, "Why, Lord, why
have you brought trouble on this people? Is this why
you sent me? Ever since I went to Pharaoh to speak
in your name, he has brought trouble on this people,
and you have not rescued your people at all."*
EXODUS 5:22–23 NIV

Moses knew the Lord set him apart to help lead the Israelites
out of Egypt. Even if it was time for the Israelites to be set
free from their bondage, the Egyptians didn't welcome
this news. In fact, Pharaoh refused to set the Israelites free,
and he increased their workload. Moses' response to these
circumstances was prayer. When he didn't understand
what was going on, he shared all the details and asked
God for clarity.

Like Moses, things may not seem to be working out the
way you'd hoped. Instead of focusing on everything that's
gone wrong, though, pray. Describe your situation to the
Lord, ask Him for help, and then wait to watch Him work.

LORD, WHY HAVE YOU LET BAD THINGS HAPPEN? I WASN'T
PREPARED FOR THE DISAPPOINTMENT AND STRUGGLE
THAT I'M FACING. PLEASE WORK IN THIS SITUATION.

SLEEPING IN SAFETY

I go to bed and sleep in peace,
because, LORD, only you keep me safe.
PSALM 4:8 NCV

If you have trouble falling asleep, it's a perfect opportunity to pray. You can toss and turn while thinking over your day and thanking God for all the good that happened, but also ask Him for help with everything that's troubling you. If you're still awake, even after you've thanked Him for His blessings, remind yourself of some of His promises. One promise is that He will keep you safe. With His safety, you can go to bed and sleep in peace. You don't have to worry.

When worries do pop into your mind, give them over to the Lord. And keep giving them over to Him until you feel at peace.

LORD, THANK YOU FOR KEEPING ME SAFE! I AM SO
GRATEFUL I CAN GO TO BED AND SLEEP IN PEACE
BECAUSE OF YOU AND YOUR CONSTANT PROTECTION.

SO SAD

Hannah was so sad that she cried and prayed to the LORD.
She made a promise, saying, "LORD All-Powerful, see how
sad I am. Remember me and don't forget me. If you will
give me a son, I will give him back to you all his life."
1 SAMUEL 1:10–11 NCV

For years, Hannah was heartbroken because she wasn't a mom. One year, as she prayed and cried in the house of the LORD, she made a promise she meant to keep. If only God would remember her and give her a son, Hannah promised to give the baby back to the Lord.

God answered Hannah's prayers and blessed her with a baby. When her son was old enough, Hannah took him to live in the house of the Lord.

Just like Hannah could cry and come to the Lord in her sadness, you can too! You always can pray, no matter how sad you feel.

LORD ALL-POWERFUL, YOU REMEMBER ME EVEN
WHEN I'M SAD. YOU WON'T EVER FORGET ME.

OPEN MY EYES

Do good to me, your servant, so I can live, so I can obey your word. Open my eyes to see the miracles in your teachings.
PSALM 119:17–18 NCV

You don't always know what the Lord is doing in your life. In fact, it might take years to figure out the ways He is working. And in some situations, you'll never understand.

When you're feeling particularly puzzled about what's going on, pray that the Lord will open your eyes to see.

It's also essential to ask Him to open your eyes to see the miracles found in His teachings in His Word. Ask Him to do good to you if it means that you will obey His Word. Read His Word so you can understand and obey it, and wait for Him to open your eyes to see the miracles in His teachings.

FATHER. PLEASE OPEN MY EYES TO SEE THE MIRACLES IN YOUR TEACHINGS. PLEASE HELP ME OBEY YOUR WORD.

ONE

"I pray for these followers, but I am also praying for all those who will believe in me because of their teaching. Father, I pray that they can be one. As you are in me and I am in you, I pray that they can also be one in us. Then the world will believe that you sent me."

JOHN 17:20–21 NCV

During Jesus' life, He spent time praying to His Father. One of the things He prayed about was you. Once Jesus left this earth, His followers' teaching about Him spread across the world. You've heard of Jesus because of His first followers.

Today, Christ followers believe the teachings of Jesus. Jesus' sincere prayer was that His followers would be one. If His followers could be one, just like Jesus and His Father were one, the world would believe that Jesus was sent by God.

You can help answer Jesus' prayer today by seeking unity with other believers. Instead of looking for differences that might divide, look for ways to stay united. Remember what you have in common: Jesus!

FATHER, I PRAY THAT I'LL STAY UNITED TO OTHER
BELIEVERS TO BRING YOU GLORY AND PRAISE.

NOT ASHAMED

Lord God All-Powerful, do not let those who hope in you be ashamed because of me. God of Israel, do not let your worshipers be disgraced because of me.

PSALM 69:6 NCV

Have you ever considered that your life choices affect other people? If you claim to follow Christ, the choices you make reflect what a Christian should live like. People will make assumptions about other believers based on what you choose to say and do.

Because this can feel really intimidating or overwhelming, it's good to pray about your witness. Pray that other believers wouldn't be ashamed because of you. Pray that the choices you make wouldn't disgrace other Christ followers. Pray for help in making the right decisions.

LORD GOD ALL-POWERFUL, I WISH MY LIFE CHOICES ONLY AFFECTED ME. BUT EVERYTHING I SAY AND DO IS A REFLECTION OF MY RELATIONSHIP WITH YOU. ALL MY CHOICES ACTUALLY MAKE A DIFFERENCE IN THE WAY THE WORLD VIEWS YOUR FOLLOWERS. PLEASE HELP ME! I DON'T WANT ANYONE TO FEEL ASHAMED BECAUSE OF ME.

NO ONE

*He said, "Lord, God of Israel, there is no god like You in heaven
or on earth, keeping Your covenant and Your faithfulness
to Your servants who walk before You with all their heart."*

2 Chronicles 6:14 nasb

God is unique. There is nothing and no one like Him in all
of history and all of the universe. He is the Creator of all. In
God, all things hold together.

When you think about who He is and you remember
how faithfully He's kept His promises, tell Him about how
awesome and amazing He is! Praise Him for who He is. Tell
Him what you appreciate most about Him, and thank Him
for being your God.

LORD GOD, THERE IS NO ONE LIKE YOU IN HEAVEN OR ON EARTH.
THANK YOU FOR KEEPING YOUR PROMISES! THANK YOU FOR
BEING SO FAITHFUL TO ME AND EVERY SINGLE ONE OF YOUR
SERVANTS. I WANT TO WALK BEFORE YOU WITH ALL MY HEART.

PROTECTED

In you, L, is my protection. Never let me be ashamed.
Because you do what is right, save and rescue me;
listen to me and save me. Be my place of safety where
I can always come. Give the command to save me,
because you are my rock and my strong, walled city.
P 71:1–3

God protects you. Whatever you face, He can be your place of safety if and when you choose to come to Him. He listens to you. He can save you and keep you from shame. He is dependable and constant, a protection from the storms of life.

While God is a strong protector, it's important to communicate with Him. Don't forget to praise Him for who He is. Recognize the many ways He protects and guides you, and thank Him for His help. Look for the ways He is working in your life, and let yourself be in awe that the God of the universe cares for you so much.

LORD. MY PROTECTION IS IN YOU. PLEASE SAVE AND
RESCUE ME. I'M SO GRATEFUL YOU ARE MY PLACE
OF SAFETY WHERE I ALWAYS CAN COME.

WHAT SHOULD I DO?

Then Moses cried out to the Lord, "What am I to do with these people? They are almost ready to stone me."
EXODUS 17:4 NIV

You never know when you might run into tricky situations or difficult people. Just when you think you have an easy day ahead of you, surprise! You may need to deal with something you never asked for or imagined.

When these challenging moments pop up throughout your life and you need to navigate what you never wanted, follow Moses' example. When he faced difficult people and conflict, he turned to God in prayer. Like Moses, frankly ask God what you should do. Tell Him the details of your situation and ask Him for help. Simply ask Him, "What should I do?"

LORD, THE SITUATION I'M FACING RIGHT NOW SEEMS SO OUT OF MY CONTROL AND SO MUCH MORE THAN I CAN HANDLE. WHAT SHOULD I DO? PLEASE HELP ME!

TO WHOM DO YOU PRAY?

*"So when you pray, you should pray like this: 'Our Father
in heaven, may your name always be kept holy.'"*
MATTHEW 6:9 NCV

During His time on earth, Jesus taught His followers many
things, including how to pray. While Jesus' example didn't
mean you could only pray using that specific prayer, it did
include a lot of powerful ways to come to the Lord.

For example, it's important to remember who you're
praying to as you pray. Remember that you're praying to
your heavenly Father. This Father is holy. He's one-of-a-kind.
You're praying to Him, and He's different from anyone and
everyone else.

Instead of praying just because you think it's the right
thing to do, remember that when you pray, you're initiating
a conversation with the Lord of all creation. Come before
Him with honor and respect, knowing that He is a perfect
God and you are an imperfect you.

MY FATHER IN HEAVEN, YOU ARE HOLY. I PRAISE YOU AND
HONOR YOU BECAUSE YOU ARE PERFECT. NO ONE IS LIKE YOU.

WHOSE WILL?

*"May your kingdom come and what you want
be done, here on earth as it is in heaven."*

MATTHEW 6:10 NCV

As Jesus taught His followers how to pray, one important part included asking the Father to have His will be done. So often, it's easy to pray and only focus on what you want to have happen. If only God could answer your every hope and wish, life would be perfect!

This idea of will is both easy and complicated. Whose will would you choose to be done? Your will? Or your heavenly Father's? Even when it's hard to realize that deep down you'd prefer God's will over your own, pray that His will might be done. That way, when you're wrestling with decisions and attitudes, you can stop and think about what His will might be in your situation. Then you can try to honor it.

HEAVENLY FATHER, MAY YOUR WILL BE DONE
IN MY LIFE AND IN THIS WORLD.

MEAL TIME!

"Give us the food we need for each day."
MATTHEW 6:11 NCV

Have you ever considered why people stop to pray and thank God before they eat a meal?

Food is essential to life. You need to eat regularly to live. And the choices of your food can make a big difference in your health, your attitude, and your energy levels. Eating too much food isn't healthy for you, and neither is eating too little.

As necessary as eating is, it's wise to remember where your food comes from. The Lord makes all things grow, including the ingredients that are needed for food. The Lord also provides resources to get the food, whether you buy it or it's given to you. The Lord works out all the little details so you can have something you need to live. Because of this, you can ask Him for food and thank Him for what He gives you.

FATHER, PLEASE GIVE ME THE FOOD I NEED TO LIVE TODAY.
AND THANK YOU FOR FAITHFULLY FEEDING ME IN THE
PAST! MAY I NEVER FORGET HOW GENEROUS YOU ARE.

FORGIVENESS

*"Forgive us for our sins, just as we have
forgiven those who sinned against us."*
MATTHEW 6:12 NCV

It's not comfortable to ask anyone for forgiveness, mainly because apologizing means you admit you've done something wrong. As a human, it's natural to love to feel like you're in the right.

You're not always right, though. Sometimes you're very wrong. Other times, you've made a big mistake.

When you know you've blown it, it's important to ask for forgiveness, both with people you've wronged and with the Lord.

As you ask your Father in heaven for forgiveness, you also can take the time to double-check if you need to forgive anyone. Has someone hurt or offended you in some way? Have they sinned against you? If that's part of your reality, it's important to forgive and not hold a grudge. Once you forgive others, you can feel free to ask for forgiveness, knowing that you're not holding on to any bitterness.

FATHER, PLEASE FORGIVE ME! I AM SO SORRY I'VE
SINNED AGAINST YOU. JUST LIKE I'M ASKING FORGIVENESS,
PLEASE HELP ME BE QUICK TO FORGIVE OTHERS AS WELL.

TEMPTATION

"And do not cause us to be tempted,
but save us from the Evil One."
MATTHEW 6:13 NCV

When Jesus taught His followers to pray, He knew the realities of life. He knew that temptation was a very real thing. Amazingly, He also was the one and only human to not give into temptation. Just because He was sinless, it didn't mean He didn't experience temptation. In fact, His temptation was very real. Jesus knew that temptation didn't come from His heavenly Father. He knew that temptation came straight from His enemy, the Evil One.

When you feel like your temptation is stronger than you can resist, pray! Pray that the Lord would remove your temptation. Pray that He might save you from the Evil One. And if your temptation doesn't disappear right away, or if it keeps popping up in your life, keep praying! Pray for strength to resist.

LORD GOD, PLEASE KEEP ME FROM TEMPTATION
AND SAVE ME FROM THE EVIL ONE.

ALL THE POWER. ALL THE GLORY

*"The kingdom, the power, and the
glory are yours forever. Amen."*
MATTHEW 6:13 NCV

When Jesus finished making requests in His model prayer, also known as the Lord's Prayer, He wrapped everything up with a reminder of who God is. God always had power, He has power right now, and He always will have power. God also is completely deserving of glory. And His kingdom has been, is, and will be His forever. Absolutely nothing can change those truths.

When you pray, think about the God to whom you're praying. Feel free to speak back all the wonderful truths you know about Him. He will reign in His kingdom forever. He is all-powerful. And He deserves your glory.

HOLY FATHER. YOUR KINGDOM IS FOREVER.
ALL POWER IS YOURS. YOU DESERVE ALL GLORY
YESTERDAY. TODAY. AND FOREVER. AMEN.

GETTING A BETTER UNDERSTANDING

Help me understand your orders.
Then I will think about your miracles.
PSALM 119:27 NCV

It can be really tough to keep in mind who God is and what He asks you to do in His Word. Whenever you have questions or His commands don't seem to make sense, ask Him to help you understand. The Lord gladly gives to those who ask, and He'll be happy to help you. Aside from prayer, one great way to try to get a better understanding is to read His Word and keep reading more and more of it. The more you read, the more things will make sense.

Once you feel like you have a better understanding of His Word, take time to consider who God is and what He's done. Every day the world is filled with His miracles. Just the fact that you woke up today and have breath in your lungs and a beating heart is pretty miraculous. Consider the miracles you've spied today and praise Him!

LORD, YOU DO AMAZING THINGS. HELP ME NOTICE THE WONDERFUL WAYS YOU WORK IN MY LIFE AND IN THIS WORLD. I WANT TO GIVE YOU CREDIT FOR ALL YOU DO!

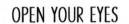

OPEN YOUR EYES

Elisha said, "Don't be afraid. The army that fights for us is larger than the one against us." Then Elisha prayed, "LORD, open my servant's eyes, and let him see." The LORD opened the eyes of the young man, and he saw that the mountain was full of horses and chariots of fire all around Elisha.

2 KINGS 6:16–17 NCV

Throughout history, God worked through specific people. One of these people who served the Lord was a man named Elisha. Once, he saw an army of angels surrounding the Israelite army. Elisha knew the Israelites had nothing to fear. No army of men could ever defeat an army of angels. To help his fellow soldier not fear, he prayed for the Lord to open his servant's eyes. God answered Elisha's prayer, and the servant saw the angel army.

When you face doubt, or your enemies are ready to fight against you, pray for the Lord's protection. Pray that you would quickly know that the Lord fights for you. His army is larger than any forces against you.

LORD, OPEN MY EYES TO SEE THAT YOU AND YOUR ARMIES ARE LARGER AND GREATER THAN ANYTHING AGAINST ME.

IN THE MIDDLE OF DISAPPOINTMENT

*Restore us, God Almighty; make your face
shine on us, that we may be saved.*

PSALM 80:7 NIV

When you're facing disappointment and discouragement, whether it's with your circumstances or your own shortcomings and sin, it's easy to realize you can't do everything on your own. These moments, even when you may feel at your lowest, are perfect opportunities to come to the Lord in prayer. After all, He is the only one who *can* do everything.

When you realize your own limitations and revere the limitless God, your life changes. Pray for Him to save you through Jesus, since you can't save yourself. Ask Him to restore you, even when it seems all is lost. Ask Him to make His face shine on you because He is God. There's nothing else in the world that compares to experiencing the Lord and His favor in that way.

GOD ALMIGHTY, PLEASE SAVE ME! PLEASE REDEEM MY
SITUATIONS AND RESTORE MY LIFE SO THAT I FIND MY
JOY IN YOU. PLEASE MAKE YOUR FACE SHINE ON ME.

A GENTLE REMINDER

*"So show your strength now, Lord. Do what you said:
'The LORD doesn't become angry quickly, but he has great
love. He forgives sin and law breaking. But the LORD never
forgets to punish guilty people. When parents sin, he will
also punish their children, their grandchildren, their great-
grandchildren, and their great-great-grandchildren.' By
your great love, forgive these people's sin, just as you have
forgiven them from the time they left Egypt until now."*

NUMBERS 14:17–19 NCV

When you need to face your fears, pray to God and remember how His Word teaches you to be strong and courageous. When you feel like you need to experience His forgiveness, tell God how you're grateful for His great love, mercy, and forgiveness. No matter how you might be feeling, remind yourself of what God has promised in His Word. Because you can rely on His promises, they're always good to remember.

LORD, YOU'RE FAITHFUL AND TRUE. YOU KEEP YOUR
PROMISES. I PRAISE YOU FOR WHAT YOU'VE PROMISED
PEOPLE WHO TRUST IN YOU. AND I PRAY YOU WILL HELP
ME LEARN MORE AND MORE OF YOUR PROMISES.

HE'S THERE

God, do not keep quiet; God, do not be silent or still.
PSALM 83:1 NCV

When it seems like God is quiet, you can begin to doubt if He's there. Does He hear your prayers? Is He involved in your life? Or have you been left on your own to figure everything out?

One of the Bible's many fantastic promises is that God will never leave you nor forsake you. Even if you don't feel Him, He's there for you. Even when it seems like He's turned His back or won't listen, He's there. He sees you. He hears you. He knows you. And He loves you.

When you're in the middle of feeling alone or questioning if He's listening, pray anyway. Like Asaph prayed in Psalm 83, ask God to not be silent or still. Ask God to reveal Himself to you in some way. Then expect to experience His work in your life.

FATHER GOD, I'M SO RELIEVED YOU'LL NEVER LEAVE OR FORSAKE ME. I DON'T LIKE IT WHEN YOU'RE SO QUIET, THOUGH. COULD YOU PLEASE LET ME KNOW YOU CARE FOR ME? COULD YOU PLEASE REMIND ME YOU'RE LISTENING TO ME AND LOVING ME?

SINGING HIS HONOR

*Then Moses and the Israelites sang this song to the
Lord: "I will sing to the Lord, because he is worthy of
great honor. He has thrown the horse and its rider into
the sea. The Lord gives me strength and makes me
sing; he has saved me. He is my God, and I will praise
him. He is the God of my ancestors, and I will honor
him. The Lord is a warrior; the Lord is his name.*
EXODUS 15:1–3 NCV

The Lord did absolutely amazing miracles that saved the
Israelites from the Egyptians. God parted the Red Sea so the
Israelites could escape on dry land, then drowned all their
Egyptian enemies. After seeing this miracle, Moses and the
Israelites sang for joy.

Just like the Israelites, you can sing for joy when you see
the Lord work in unmistakable, unbelievable ways. Praise
Him! Pray by retelling all that God has done in your life,
and then thank Him for what His great works mean to you.

LORD, YOU ARE WORTHY OF GREAT HONOR! YOU GIVE
ME STRENGTH. YOU MAKE ME SING. YOU HAVE SAVED
ME! YOU ARE MY GOD, AND I WILL PRAISE YOU.

WHO HE IS

*Lord our Lord, your name is the most wonderful name
in all the earth! It brings you praise in heaven above.
You have taught children and babies to sing praises to
you because of your enemies. And so you silence your
enemies and destroy those who try to get even.*

PSALM 8:1–2 NCV

It's easy to think that life is all about yourself. You're uniquely
made, and there's only one you. Yet as important as you are,
and as much as you think of yourself, you're one of many
humans throughout history. Even the most amazing people
who have ever existed are humans who are born and die.

God, though, is different. He has always and will always
exist. In Him all things are held together. Because of who
He is, His name is the most wonderful name in all the earth.
More than anything or anyone, He deserves praise. As you
pray, remember who He is. Remember that He is God, and
there is none other like Him.

LORD MY LORD, YOUR NAME IS THE MOST WONDERFUL
NAME IN ALL THE EARTH! I PRAISE YOU!

WHAT IF?

Then Abraham approached him and asked, "Do you plan to destroy the good people along with the evil ones? What if there are fifty good people in that city? Will you still destroy it? Surely you will save the city for the fifty good people living there. Surely you will not destroy the good people along with the evil ones."

GENESIS 18:23–25 NCV

Abraham knew the Lord. He talked with Him and experienced His fulfilled promises. When God told Abraham He would destroy Sodom and Gomorrah, Abraham reasoned that if fifty good people lived there, the cities would be worth saving.

Because God sees the hearts of every person, He knew that not even fifty good people lived in those cities. He knew they were evil. Yet He still considered Abraham's plea.

Even though you don't know what's in the hearts of others, you can pray for them to turn from their ways and seek the one true God who can save them.

LORD GOD ALMIGHTY, YOU ARE THE JUDGE OF ALL THE EARTH. I TRUST THAT YOU ALWAYS DO WHAT IS RIGHT. PLEASE HELP OTHERS BEGIN TO TRUST THAT TOO.

BUT WHAT IF?

Then Abraham said, "Though I am only dust and ashes,
I have been brave to speak to the Lord. What if there are
only forty-five good people in the city? Will you destroy
the whole city for the lack of five good people?" The LORD
said, "If I find forty-five there, I will not destroy the city."
GENESIS 18:27–28 NCV

Abraham questioned the Lord about being merciful to even fifty good people in Sodom and Gomorrah. But when the Lord knew that not even fifty good people lived there, Abraham gathered up his courage to ask again. Would the Lord show mercy to the cities if forty-five good people lived there?

God entertained Abraham's question. He didn't take offense. And He considered it.

Like Abraham, you can ask God similar requests with great respect and honor. Through your prayers, try to discern the will of God.

LORD, I'M JUST A PERSON. PRAYING TO YOU IS A GIFT.
BUT IT ALSO REQUIRES SOME BRAVERY. I PRAY YOU'LL LISTEN
TO MY REQUESTS FOR OTHERS. NO MATTER WHAT YOUR
ANSWER IS, I KNOW I CAN COME TO YOU IN PRAYER.

FILLED WITH JOY

Hannah prayed: "The Lord has filled my heart with joy; I feel very strong in the Lord. I can laugh at my enemies; I am glad because you have helped me! There is no one holy like the Lord. There is no God but you; there is no Rock like our God."
1 Samuel 2:1–2 NCV

Hannah felt utterly helpless. She was married without children, even though her sincere hope was to become a mother. In her despair and heartbreak, she did what mattered: she cried and prayed to the Lord for help.

God answered Hannah's pleas! She had a son. When she knew God answered her prayers, she prayed again to thank Him for His help. She was filled with joy and knew that there was no one like God. She knew He was holy. She knew He was her Rock.

Like Hannah, thank God when you know He answers your prayers. Celebrate your joy! And praise your holy God, because there is no one like Him. He is your Rock.

THERE IS NO ONE HOLY LIKE YOU, LORD.
THERE IS NO GOD BUT YOU. YOU ARE MY ROCK!

HELP IN THE HURT

*I cry to you for help, LORD; in the morning my
prayer comes before you. Why, LORD, do you
reject me and hide your face from me?*

PSALM 88:13–14 NIV

When you're hurting, don't try to fix things on your own.
Don't rush to someone else to try to ease your pain. Even if
you want someone else's reassurance or encouragement or
ideas on what to do, just wait. Instead of turning to things
in this world to try to make you feel better, stop.

When you're hurting, turn first to the Lord. Before you
seek anyone else or try to rely on your own methods of
comfort, ask the Lord for help. Cry out to Him. Pray to Him.
Ask Him why you're facing what you're facing. Ask Him to
help you.

He may bring other people along to help. He may bring
solutions your way. But before you reach out on your own,
pray to Him first.

HELP ME, LORD! I DON'T KNOW WHY I NEED TO FACE WHAT I'M
GOING THROUGH, BUT I'M ASKING YOU TO PLEASE HELP!

WORTHY!

In a loud voice they were saying: "Worthy is the Lamb,
who was slain, to receive power and wealth and wisdom
and strength and honor and glory and praise!"
REVELATION 5:12 NIV

From what the Bible reveals about heaven, there's going to be one massive focus: praising the Lord! According to Revelation 5, twenty-four elders worship the Lord while holding golden bowls full of the prayers of God's people. As they worship the Lord, they sing praises. Thousands of angels join in the praise, speaking about the Lord's worthiness. They tell how He is worthy to receive power and wealth and wisdom and strength and honor and glory and praise.

Like the angels, you can say the same things to God right now. Praise Him! Tell Him that He alone is worthy to receive power and wealth and wisdom and strength and honor and glory and praise. Because He is.

LORD, YOU ALONE ARE WORTHY! YOU ARE WORTHY
OF ALL MY HONOR. YOU ARE WORTHY OF ALL
GLORY. YOU ARE WORTHY OF ALL MY PRAISE.

YOUR TRUE HOME

Lord, you have been our home since the beginning.
Before the mountains were born and before you
created the earth and the world, you are God.
You have always been, and you will always be.
PSALM 90:1–2 NCV

So often it feels like there's no place like home. But what if your true home is with the Lord? It makes sense that there's truly no place like home when He is your home.

Moses knew there is no one like God. And when he wrote Psalm 90, he shared what he knew to be true: God always has been. God always will be. He created everything, including the earth.

Before God created all of creation, He was your home. Spend today pondering this and praising God that He truly is your home. The belongings you'll gather in this life will never measure up to Him, your true home.

LORD. YOU HAVE BEEN MY HOME SINCE THE BEGINNING.
WHAT A SWEET RELIEF AND BLESSING!

YOU KNOW! PLEASE SHOW

The apostles prayed, "Lord, you know the thoughts of
everyone. Show us which one of these two you have chosen
to do this work. Show us who should be an apostle in place
of Judas, who turned away and went where he belongs."
ACTS 1:24–25 NCV

When you're facing a big decision and you aren't sure what choice is best, you can ask other people for input and opinions. But before you decide anything, make sure you ask the Lord!

When the disciples needed to choose a replacement for Judas Iscariot, two men seemed like obvious choices. To keep their group at only twelve members, only one of the two could be chosen. Who should the disciples pick?

The disciples didn't know what was truly in the hearts and minds of the two men. So they prayed the Lord would show them the right choice.

Like the disciples, you can ask the Lord to let you know who or what He's chosen to do in your life.

LORD, YOU KNOW THE THOUGHTS OF EVERYONE.
PLEASE SHOW ME HOW YOU HAVE CHOSEN TO DO THE
WORK IN MY LIFE. PLEASE SHOW ME WHAT I SHOULD DO!

IT IS GOOD!

*It is good to give thanks to the Lᴏʀᴅ and to sing praises
to Your name, Most High; to declare Your goodness
in the morning and Your faithfulness by night.*
Pꜱᴀʟᴍ 92:1–2 ɴᴀꜱʙ

The psalmist knew it was good to thank the Lord and sing praises to Him. The psalmist knew it was good to consider and talk about the Lord's goodness every morning and His faithfulness every night.

One great way to start your day is to pray. You can praise the Lord, ask Him for His guidance and help in your day, and remember how very good He is. You can pray throughout your day when you need help, or you feel like talking with your Father. At the end of the day, when you're getting ready to fall asleep, you can think over your day and thank God for the way He faithfully worked in your life.

FATHER, YOU ARE GOOD! YOU ARE WORTHY OF MY PRAISE.
THANK YOU FOR BEING SO FAITHFUL TO ME.

GIVE ME SUCCESS

*"Lord, listen carefully to the prayer of your servant
and the prayers of your servants who love to
honor you. Give me, your servant, success today;
allow this king to show kindness to me."*

NEHEMIAH 1:11 NCV

Nehemiah, a servant of King Artaxerxes, knew he needed to help the Jews in Jerusalem. The trouble was, he was far from Jerusalem and was busy with his work responsibilities. He would need to ask the king to take a leave to do the Lord's work. Asking the king to take a break was intimidating, though. What would the response be?

Before he said a word to the king, Nehemiah wept, fasted, and prayed. Ultimately, he asked the Lord to give him success with the king.

God answered the prayer. Nehemiah found favor with the king and was able to return to Jerusalem.

Like Nehemiah, if you need to talk with someone in authority about something important and you're afraid, pray! Ask the Lord for strength. Ask the Lord for success.

LORD, LISTEN CAREFULLY TO MY PRAYER. I LOVE TO HONOR
YOU. PLEASE GIVE ME, YOUR SERVANT, SUCCESS TODAY!

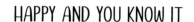

HAPPY AND YOU KNOW IT

I will praise you, Lord, with all my heart. I will tell all the
miracles you have done. I will be happy because of
you; God Most High, I will sing praises to your name.
PSALM 9:1–2 NCV

How do you feel when people tell you all the wonderful things they love about you? When someone else tells you how much they appreciate you and exactly why, doesn't it brighten your day?

Just like you feel good when someone praises you, it's important to tell God all the wonderful things you love about Him. Tell Him exactly why you're thankful for Him. Think about all the things He's done in your life that you're grateful for. Consider what you appreciate most about Him, and then tell Him. He will love to hear your gratitude and praises!

WITH ALL MY HEART, I PRAISE YOU, LORD!
I AM HAPPY BECAUSE OF YOU. I'M SO THANKFUL
FOR ALL THE MIRACLES YOU HAVE DONE.

NO ONE LIKE HIM

"There is no one like you, Lord, and there is no God but you, as we have heard with our own ears."

1 Chronicles 17:20 niv

Consider who the God of the universe is: He made all things. He's all-knowing. Even if you can't see Him, He's always present. He's all-powerful too. He created all things, and in Him all things hold together. (Not just some things but *all* things!) He is full of love and compassion. He forgives and pours out undeserved mercy. His kindness and love endure forever. He has a plan and purpose for everything. He always has existed and always will exist. There is no one like Him.

As you consider who God is, praise Him! Marvel at what your mind can't fully understand and worship Him. He deserves your praise and adoration!

LORD, THERE IS NO ONE LIKE YOU!
I PRAISE YOU FOR WHO YOU ARE.

MERCY!

Lord, have mercy on me. See how my enemies hurt me. Do not let me go through the gates of death. Then, at the gates of Jerusalem, I will praise you; I will rejoice because you saved me.
PSALM 9:13–14 NCV

If life seems harder than it should be, you may wish that someone would have pity on you. What if God had pity on you? What if He would work in your life and bring some of His limitless compassion?

If you wish God would show you His pity, compassion, and mercy, ask Him for it! You can go into the details of whatever's upsetting you, or you also can keep your request as simple as asking the Lord to have mercy on you.

When He does act in mercy and change your situation, be sure to thank Him with joy. Rejoice when He saves you!

LORD, HAVE MERCY ON ME. PLEASE SAVE ME FROM THE SITUATION THAT IS UPSETTING ME SO MUCH. I'M GLAD I CAN TRUST YOU!

GLORY TO GOD

Glory to God who can make you strong in faith by the Good News that I tell people and by the message about Jesus Christ. The message about Christ is the secret that was hidden for long ages past but is now made known. . . . And by the command of the eternal God it is made known to all nations that they might believe and obey. To the only wise God be glory forever through Jesus Christ! Amen.

ROMANS 16:25–27 NCV

When you give glory to something or someone, you show honor and praise. You lift, or glorify, someone if you acknowledge their fame.

Think about who God is, all He's done, and all He will do for people who believe His message about Jesus Christ. He deserves belief and obedience. He also deserves all the glory you can give. You can give Him glory, honor, and praise right now in your prayers.

ONLY WISE GOD, TO YOU BE GLORY FOREVER
THROUGH JESUS CHRIST! AMEN.

RISE UP!

Lord, rise up and judge the nations. Don't let people
think they are strong. Teach them to fear you, Lord.
The nations must learn that they are only human.
PSALM 9:19–20 NCV

It can be really frustrating and discouraging to look at the
world around you and notice all the people who turn their
backs on the Lord. You might feel like they get away with
celebrating their own sins without any consequences. You
may wonder how evil can take hold of so many people,
choices, and situations.

When you notice all the evil and sin, don't keep it to
yourself. Talk to the Lord about it. Tell Him how it makes you
feel. Get all the confusion and anger and fear and frustration
out of your head and turn it over to God. As you do, don't
be afraid if some of your processing sounds angry. Ask the
Lord to judge what's wrong. Get it all out, and then leave
it in the Lord's hands. He sees what's going on. He knows.
And He will act.

LORD, RISE UP AND TEACH UNBELIEVERS TO FEAR YOU. WRECK EVIL
PLANS BEFORE PEOPLE FOLLOW THROUGH AND ACT ON THEM.

TURN AND RELENT

*But Moses sought the favor of the Lord his God.
"Lord," he said, "why should your anger burn against
your people, whom you brought out of Egypt with great
power and a mighty hand? Why should the Egyptians
say, 'It was with evil intent that he brought them out,
to kill them in the mountains and to wipe them off
the face of the earth'? Turn from your fierce anger;
relent and do not bring disaster on your people."*
EXODUS 32:11–12 NIV

God is justified to punish sin. When He's angry, He can act
with great power. If you sin and decide to change your ways
through repentance and ask for forgiveness, don't be afraid
to ask God to withhold His judgment and discipline from
you. Ask Him to turn from His anger and hope that He will
choose to show mercy.

LORD, PLEASE TURN FROM YOUR FIERCE ANGER. IN MERCY,
PLEASE DO NOT BRING DISASTER TO YOUR PEOPLE.

ENCOURAGE, LISTEN, AND DEFEND

You, Lord, hear the desire of the afflicted;
you encourage them, and you listen to their cry,
defending the fatherless and the oppressed, so that
mere earthly mortals will never again strike terror.
PSALM 10:17–18 NIV

In Psalm 10, the psalmist's prayer reflected all the amazing things God does for the persecuted and abandoned. God not only hears the desires of the afflicted, but He also encourages them. God not only listens to the cries of the fatherless and oppressed, but He also defends them.

As you notice the afflicted in your community, pray for them. See if you can partner with the Lord and encourage them in any way. As you see people who are oppressed, pray for them too. Look for ways to defend them with a helpful, loving heart. Definitely pray and, if at all possible, definitely act.

LORD, PLEASE HEAR AND ENCOURAGE THE AFFLICTED.
PLEASE DEFEND THE FATHERLESS AND OPPRESSED,
AND PLEASE GIVE ME OPPORTUNITIES TO DO THE SAME.

ALWAYS

Then Jesus looked up and said, "Father, I thank you that you heard me. I know that you always hear me, but I said these things because of the people here around me. I want them to believe that you sent me."
JOHN 11:41–42 NCV

Jesus spent a lot of His time on earth praying to His heavenly Father. Often He woke up before anyone else did just so He could go off by Himself and pray. He knew that God listened to His prayers.

When He prayed out loud in front of other people, sometimes He intentionally taught certain things. For example, when He thanked His Father for hearing Him, He explained that He already knew that His Father hears and listens. Jesus said it just so other people would hear and believe that God the Father heard Him.

Just like Jesus knew that His Father always heard His prayers, you can have the same assurance. God hears you. Always.

FATHER, I THANK YOU THAT YOU HEAR ME.
THANK YOU FOR SENDING JESUS.

CREATOR

Lord, you have made many things; with your wisdom you made them all. The earth is full of your riches. . . . All these things depend on you to give them their food at the right time. When you give it to them, they gather it up. When you open your hand, they are filled with good food.

PSALM 104:24, 27–28 NCV

Look around and try to find as many things as you can that the Lord has made. What do you spy? From flowers and trees to animals and bees, God has created every living thing. Keep looking and you'll notice the sky and the sun. And take a moment to look at your body. Study your hands and fingers and you'll find all kinds of miracles made by God.

When you take time to slow down and study what He created, it's easy to notice His creativity, unmatched genius, and amazing artistry. Now that you've considered this, tell Him how impressed and amazed you are! Praise Him for what you specifically appreciate.

LORD, YOU HAVE MADE MANY THINGS.
WITH YOUR ASTOUNDING ABILITY AND WONDERFUL
WISDOM YOU MADE THEM ALL.

ASKING FOR DIRECTIONS

Later, David prayed to the LORD, saying, "Should I go up to any of the cities of Judah?" The LORD said to David, "Go." David asked, "Where should I go?" The LORD answered, "To Hebron."
2 SAMUEL 2:1 NCV

David was considered a man after God's heart, and the verse in 2 Samuel reveals why: he asked God for direction, guidance, and clarity, and then he obeyed God. Because he did whatever God asked him to do, he was a man after God's heart.

You can be a young woman after God's heart by following David's example and asking God what to do and then obeying His direction. The alternative is listening to yourself and doing your own thing. Each time you listen to the world's advice to follow your own heart, you turn away from becoming a woman after God's heart. Start following the Lord by asking Him what you should do, finding direction in His Word, and then doing it.

LORD. SHOULD I GO AND DO CERTAIN THINGS?
AND IF SO. WHERE SHOULD I GO? WHAT SHOULD I DO?
HELP ME BECOME A WOMAN AFTER YOUR HEART.

PAY ATTENTION

*Lord, listen to my prayer; let my cry for
help come to you. Do not hide from me in
my time of trouble. Pay attention to me.
When I cry for help, answer me quickly.*
PSALM 102:1–2 NCV

When you're upset and confide in someone you trust, you want to make sure they're listening to you. You want to know that they care. Just like this is true in your relationships with people, it's true in your relationship with God.

The psalmist felt the same way when he wanted to make sure God was listening to his prayer. He wanted to know that the Lord was paying attention to his cry for help. He didn't want the Lord to hide from him, especially when it felt like he was in trouble.

Like the psalmist, you can ask God to listen to your prayer. When you're facing trouble, cry out to Him for help and ask Him to pay attention to you.

LORD, LISTEN TO MY PRAYER. PLEASE DON'T HIDE FROM
ME IN MY TIME OF TROUBLE. PAY ATTENTION TO ME.

FAVOR

"Now then, if I have found favor in Your sight in any way, please let me know Your ways so that I may know You, in order that I may find favor in Your sight. Consider too, that this nation is Your people." And He said, "My presence shall go with you, and I will give you rest." Then he said to Him, "If Your presence does not go with us, do not lead us up from here. For how then can it be known that I have found favor in Your sight, I and Your people?"
EXODUS 33:13–16 NASB

Because Moses was a friend of God, he knew God's character. He knew he could ask if he found favor with God. And he knew that he needed to know God's ways. By knowing God, he could better find favor in the Lord's sight.

Start learning the ways of God so you can know Him and find favor in His sight.

LORD. IF I HAVE FOUND FAVOR IN YOUR SIGHT IN ANY WAY. PLEASE LET ME KNOW YOUR WAYS SO THAT I MAY KNOW YOU. I WANT TO FIND FAVOR IN YOUR SIGHT.

I AM NOT AFRAID

*Thousands of troops may surround me, but I
am not afraid. Lord, rise up! My God, come save
me! You have struck my enemies on the cheek;
you have broken the teeth of the wicked.*

PSALM 3:6–7 NCV

At times in your life, you'll feel like you're surrounded by enemies. It doesn't need to be thousands against you like David wrote in Psalm 3, but dealing with any enemy can make you feel awful. It doesn't feel comfortable to know you disagree with someone. And it can feel scary or intimidating to know someone opposes you.

No matter what enemy you're dealing with, you don't have to be afraid if you have the Lord in your life. He can save you. He can punish your enemies and protect you. He can rise up as your defender and shield. All you need to do is ask Him.

BECAUSE OF YOU, LORD, I AM NOT AFRAID. RISE UP AND SAVE ME!

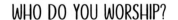

WHO DO YOU WORSHIP?

"When my life had almost gone, I remembered the
LORD. I prayed to you, and you heard my prayers in
your Holy Temple. People who worship useless idols
give up their loyalty to you. But I will praise and thank
you while I give sacrifices to you, and I will keep my
promises to you. Salvation comes from the LORD!"
JONAH 2:7–9 NCV

Everyone worships something. Whether you worship your belongings or ideals or people, it's easy to devote your attention, honor, and praise to something other than God. Because it's so easy, the Bible is filled with warnings against worshipping things other than God.

When you want to keep your worship and devotion focused on the one true God, remember who He is. Think about His power and might. Remember He is holy. There is no one like Him. After you've thought about Him, pray to Him and tell Him everything that is worthy of your worship.

FATHER. I NEVER WANT TO GIVE UP MY LOYALTY TO YOU. I PRAISE
AND THANK YOU AND WANT TO KEEP MY PROMISES TO YOU.

RISE UP! STAND UP! GET UP!

*Lord, rise up in your anger; stand up against my
enemies' anger. Get up and demand fairness.*
PSALM 7:6 NCV

If the Lord is on your side, you are never alone. And you
never need to be afraid. But if you do find yourself facing
fearful situations, you can pray against that fear. Like the
psalmist demonstrated, ask God to rise up in His anger to
repay what needs to be done. Ask Him to stand up against
your enemies. Ask Him to get up and demand fairness.

Once you pray for God to work, relax. Try to live in
fairness and not out of anger. Let your heavenly Father do
His good work by defending you.

LORD, I LONG FOR YOUR FAIRNESS. WOULD YOU PLEASE
RISE UP AND STAND FOR ME? PLEASE GET UP TO DEMAND
FAIRNESS AND STAND AGAINST MY ENEMIES' ANGER.

THANK YOU!

*Simeon took the baby in his arms and thanked
God: "Now, Lord, you can let me, your servant,
die in peace as you said. With my own eyes I have
seen your salvation, which you prepared before all
people. It is a light for the non-Jewish people to see
and an honor for your people, the Israelites."*
LUKE 2:28–32 NCV

In the New Testament, Simeon was a righteous and devout Jew who was waiting to see the Messiah. When Mary and Joseph took baby Jesus into the temple, Simeon knew right away that this baby was the one he had been waiting for. Here was the Messiah as a precious baby.

After seeing the answer to his prayers right before his eyes, Simeon's response was praise through prayers to God. He made sure to thank God right away.

When you recognize an answered prayer in your own life, be like Simeon. Stop everything and thank God. The Lord is worthy of your praise!

LORD, YOU ARE SO GOOD TO ANSWER PRAYERS AND FULFILL YOUR
PROMISES. I DON'T EVER WANT TO TAKE ANY OF THAT FOR GRANTED.

TROUBLE TIMES

Lord, rise up and punish the wicked.
Don't forget those who need help.
Psalm 10:12 NCV

For the psalmists, facing a lot of opposition and challenging people was a huge distraction. The wicked relentlessly created trouble. But instead of taking revenge into their own hands, the psalmists trusted in the Lord. They knew He would know and remember His children needed help. He could rise up and punish the wicked.

When you find yourself in situations you'd rather avoid, or if trouble seems to keep popping up in your life, talk to God about it. If specific problem people are stirring up trouble, ask God to take care of the situation for you. He can rise up. And He can punish.

FATHER. WOULD YOU PLEASE REMEMBER YOUR CHILDREN WHO NEED HELP? I'M FACING A LOT OF TROUBLE CAUSED BY OTHER PEOPLE. COULD YOU PLEASE RISE UP AND JUDGE THOSE WHO ARE WRONG? COULD YOU PLEASE PUNISH THE WICKED?

PRAISE HIM!

Then Solomon stood before the altar of the Lord in front of the whole assembly of Israel, spread out his hands toward heaven and said: "Lord, the God of Israel, there is no God like you in heaven above or on earth below—you who keep your covenant of love with your servants who continue wholeheartedly in your way."

1 Kings 8:22–23 niv

For years, the Israelites wandered and lived without a temple of the Lord. When it finally was constructed during King Solomon's reign, the completion called for a huge celebration. Solomon made sure that praise and prayer were a major focus throughout the festivities, because God faithfully allowed and enabled the work to be finished.

Just as Solomon recognized that God was the driving force behind the entire project, you also can look for the ways God is working mightily in your own life. When you see Him working, thank Him! When you notice fantastic things He's bringing about, praise Him!

LORD. THERE IS NO GOD LIKE YOU IN HEAVEN ABOVE OR ON EARTH BELOW. I PRAISE YOU FOR YOUR GOOD WORK!

SAVE ME!

Save me, Lord, because the good people are all gone;
no true believers are left on earth. Everyone lies to his
neighbors; they say one thing and mean another.

PSALM 12:1–2 NCV

Ever feel like all the good people are gone? When you look around and see evil thriving and bad behavior being celebrated, it's easy to feel alone. Are you the only one who cares about living a life that pleases God? Is evil triumphing over good?

Surprisingly, this feeling of good versus evil has always been the case. David certainly felt like he was the only true believer around when he wrote Psalm 12. He could see sin multiplying around him—people were mean, deceitful liars.

Sadly, not much has changed. When you feel like you're the only true believer around, pray to the Lord. Ask Him to save you and protect you from the evil that's around you.

SAVE ME, LORD! PLEASE SHOW ME WHERE OTHER TRUE
BELIEVERS ARE SO I WON'T FEEL SO ALONE.

KEEPING IT REAL

But Moses said to the LORD, "Please, Lord, I have never been a skilled speaker. Even now, after talking to you, I cannot speak well. I speak slowly and can't find the best words."
EXODUS 4:10 NCV

You never know when God will give you an opportunity to do His good work, even when you feel unqualified, unprepared, or unworthy. Moses felt that way when God asked Him to speak for the Israelites. In fact, Moses told God through prayer that he didn't think he could do the job. Instead of trusting God in faith, Moses listed all the excuses that were standing in his way.

God can do anything. With Him, all things are possible. When He gives you a job to do, you can pray and talk to Him about your limitations. But you also can choose to trust Him and watch Him work all the details out.

LORD, I WANT TO TRUST YOU, EVEN WHEN YOU ASK ME TO DO WHAT FEELS IMPOSSIBLE. NOTHING IS IMPOSSIBLE FOR YOU!

WATCH YOUR WORDS

LORD, help me control my tongue; help me be
careful about what I say. Take away my desire
to do evil or to join others in doing wrong.
PSALM 141:3–4 NCV

Are you in the habit of speaking before you think? Do you just say whatever comes to mind without considering your words first? You might think it's good to transparently share whatever's on your mind. But people can feel hurt if you don't consider what you're saying.

Unfortunately, you can't take back words that have been spoken. If you've hurt someone by what you've said, the damage already is done.

To prevent that kind of harm from happening in the future, try to think before you say something. But you also can go a step further and ask the Lord to help you control your tongue. Pray that He would help you be careful about what you say. And when He answers your prayers and you feel like you shouldn't say something, keep quiet!

LORD, HELP ME CONTROL MY TONGUE!
PLEASE HELP ME BE CAREFUL ABOUT WHAT I SAY.

PRAYING WITH EMOTION

While Ezra was praying and confessing, weeping and throwing himself down before the house of God, a large crowd of Israelites—men, women and children—gathered around him. They too wept bitterly.

EZRA 10:1 NIV

For many people, prayer seems like something that's done quickly before a meal or during a church service. But prayer includes so much more than that. As a conversation with the Lord, when you pray through intense topics and situations, you can't help but get emotional. In the Old Testament, Ezra prayed. And as he confessed his sins and the sins of the Israelites to the Lord, he couldn't help but weep bitterly. That's confession and repentance: being truly sorry and grieved by your sin.

Don't forget to really think during your prayer times. Consider what you're praying about. If and when you get emotional, get emotional. Be all in, physically, mentally, emotionally, and spiritually, to whatever you're saying to the Lord.

FATHER, I DON'T WANT TO TAKE MY CONVERSATIONS WITH YOU FOR GRANTED. PLEASE HELP ME PONDER AND UNDERSTAND EXACTLY WHAT I'M SAYING TO YOU AND EXACTLY WHAT I'M ASKING.

PRECIOUS PROTECTION

God, your love is so precious! You protect
people in the shadow of your wings.
PSALM 36:7 NCV

God's love is such a good, precious gift. Not everyone chooses to experience it. The same is true of His protection. He pours out His protection on people, and just like birds protect their young under the cover of their wings, God will do the same for you. But some people decide to turn their back on God, ignoring His love and protection.

When you feel His love and recognize His protection, be sure to thank Him. Tell Him what you love and appreciate about Him! Consider all of the very good things He does in you and for you, and then tell Him how you feel. Praise Him!

GOD, YOU ARE SO VERY GOOD TO ME! YOUR LOVE IS ABSOLUTELY PRECIOUS. IT'S ONE OF THE BEST THINGS IN MY LIFE. AND BECAUSE YOU PROTECT ME, I HAVE NOTHING TO FEAR. THANK YOU!

LISTEN

*The Lord came and stood there, calling as at the
other times, "Samuel! Samuel!" Then Samuel
said, "Speak, for your servant is listening."*
1 Samuel 3:10 niv

Samuel was dedicated to serving the Lord with his life since before he was born. As a boy, he grew up ministering to the Lord by helping Eli the priest. Samuel actually slept in the house of the Lord, and one night the Lord clearly spoke to him.

When Samuel first thought Eli was calling him, Eli assured Samuel it must be the Lord. When the Lord called for Samuel again, Samuel had an excellent response: "Speak, for your servant is listening."

If you've been trying to discern God's will for your life and have been coming to the Lord in prayer, ask Him to speak. Tell Him that you, His servant, are listening, and then listen. Keep serving Him, keep waiting for Him, and listen.

SPEAK, LORD, FOR YOUR SERVANT IS LISTENING.

DISTRACTED

*Keep me from looking at worthless
things. Let me live by your word.*
PSALM 119:37 NCV

So much in this world is eye-catching. But how many of these desirable-looking things are simply distractions? How much of what you see and hear and think about is not very worthwhile?

It can feel impossible to avoid focusing on things that will not last. After living in a world of distractions, how can you narrow your focus on what truly matters? How can you train yourself to think about things that are lasting? How can you start considering what's eternal?

The best way to begin to switch your focus is to pray about it. Ask God to help you stop looking at worthless things. Ask Him to help you think about what's true and lasting. You may need to ask Him several times a day—or even several times an hour! It's okay! The important thing is that you ask Him for help and then follow through in obedience.

LORD, I LIVE IN A WORLD OF DISTRACTIONS.
PLEASE KEEP ME FROM LOOKING AT WORTHLESS THINGS.
PLEASE KEEP ME FOCUSED ON WHAT TRULY MATTERS.

THE FLEECE

Gideon said to God, "If you will save Israel by my hand as you have promised—look, I will place a wool fleece on the threshing floor. If there is dew only on the fleece and all the ground is dry, then I will know that you will save Israel by my hand, as you said." And that is what happened. Gideon rose early the next day; he squeezed the fleece and wrung out the dew—a bowlful of water.

JUDGES 6:36–38 NIV

Gideon, a humble son of a farmer, was asked to be a brave and mighty warrior. He didn't understand how this could be possible, but Gideon was willing to obey. Before he jumped into action, though, he wanted to make sure he accurately understood the Lord. In prayer, Gideon asked the Lord to confirm the assignment.

If, like Gideon, you find yourself needing to do something big for the Lord, you may want to make sure you're understanding Him correctly. Ask the Lord for clarity. He'll provide it in some way!

FATHER, PLEASE MAKE IT OBVIOUS WHEN I NEED TO DO SOMETHING FOR YOU SO THAT I HAVE NO REASON TO DOUBT YOUR WILL.

PRAISE! HONOR! GLORY! POWER!

*Then I heard all creatures in heaven and on earth and
under the earth and in the sea saying: "To the One
who sits on the throne and to the Lamb be praise and
honor and glory and power forever and ever."*
REVELATION 5:13 NCV

The final book in the Bible, Revelation, gives us a peek into
what heaven is like. While not many specifics are given, one
thing is certain: there will be lots and lots of praise! All creatures will praise the Lord—creatures in heaven, creatures on
earth, creatures under the earth, and creatures in the sea.
All will acknowledge that praise, honor, glory, and power
be given to God forever and ever.

You can get the praise started in your own life right now.
Praise the Lord! He deserves all praise, all honor, all glory.
And He has all power not just today but forever and ever.

LORD GOD, YOU ARE WORTHY OF MY PRAISE! YOU ARE WORTHY
OF MY HONOR. YOU ARE WORTHY OF ALL GLORY. YOU HAVE
ALL POWER. I WANT TO PRAISE YOU FOREVER AND EVER!

LISTEN AND UNDERSTAND

Lord, listen to my words. Understand my sadness. Listen to my cry for help, my King and my God, because I pray to you.
PSALM 5:1–2 NCV

No one can feel the intensity of your feelings like you do. Even if people will never fully understand, you still can ask the Lord to listen to your words as you pray. Tell Him how you're feeling. When you feel happy, tell Him. When you're sad, explain how you feel and why you feel that way. Ask God to understand your sadness. And ask Him for comfort.

Remember that, like David, you're praying to God the King. He can and will listen to your cry for help. When you feel helpless, He is the only one who can make a difference.

LORD. LISTEN TO MY WORDS. UNDERSTAND MY SADNESS. PLEASE LISTEN TO MY CRY FOR HELP! I AM SO GRATEFUL I CAN PRAY TO YOU. MY KING AND MY GOD.

THE MIRACULOUS

And he called to the Lord and said, "Lord, my God, have You also brought catastrophe upon the widow with whom I am staying, by causing her son to die?" Then he. . .called to the Lord and said, "Lord, my God, please, let this boy's life return to him." And the Lord listened to the voice of Elijah, and the life of the boy returned to him and he revived.

1 KINGS 17:20–22 NASB

You pray to a God of miracles! The Bible is filled with details of how men and women prayed, trusted God in faith, and witnessed miracles.

For example, the prophet Elijah was friends with a widow and her son. When the son died unexpectedly, Elijah prayed to the Lord, asking for God to let the boy's life return. The Lord listened, and the boy came back to life.

As you pray, ask for what seems like it's impossible. Keep worshipping Him, seeking Him, living in obedience to His Word, and trusting Him by faith. You never know what He might do!

LORD, MY GOD, MAY I NEVER FORGET THAT WHEN I PRAY
TO YOU, I'M PRAYING TO THE GOD OF MIRACLES.

STOP AND TRUST

Lord my God, I trust in you for protection.
Save me and rescue me from those who are chasing
me. Otherwise, like a lion they will tear me apart.
They will rip me to pieces, and no one can save me.
PSALM 7:1–2 NCV

When you feel especially afraid about all the things that might happen, stop yourself. Choose to stop thinking of all the what ifs and talk to God about them. Choose to trust Him for protection.

When you can't stop thinking about what might go wrong, stop yourself. Choose to not think about an unknown future. Choose to put the past behind you. Choose to focus on right now. What is God doing for you right at this moment? In what ways is He protecting you? For what circumstances do you need to trust Him?

Instead of letting yourself get overwhelmed with all that might happen, stop and remember all that He is. He is the God worthy of your trust.

FATHER, IT'S SO EASY TO GET CAUGHT IN OBSESSING OVER ALL THAT MIGHT HAPPEN. PLEASE HELP ME TRUST YOU MORE AND MORE.

SHINE BRIGHT

But whenever Moses went in before the Lord to speak
with Him, he would take off the veil until he came out;
and whenever he came out and spoke to the sons
of Israel what he had been commanded, the sons of
Israel would see the face of Moses, that the skin of
Moses' face shone. So Moses would put the veil back
over his face until he went in to speak with Him.

EXODUS 34:34–35 NASB

When you spend time with your heavenly Father, it changes you from the inside out. The more time you spend with Him and the more He changes your heart, the more noticeable your outward changes will be. As His peace, love, and joy fill your heart, you can't help but radiate His goodness. You can't help but shine.

Spend time in prayer and shine bright, daughter of God.

LORD, I WANT TO SPEND TIME WITH YOU! IT'S FASCINATING TO
KNOW THAT THE MORE TIME I SPEND WITH YOU, THE MORE YOU
WILL CHANGE ME AND THE BRIGHTER I WILL SHINE FOR YOU.

REMEMBER

In you, Lord my God, I put my trust. I trust in you;
do not let me be put to shame, nor let my enemies
triumph over me. No one who hopes in you will
ever be put to shame, but shame will come on
those who are treacherous without cause.

PSALM 25:1–3 NIV

When you pray, it can be helpful to remind yourself of who God is. Exactly who is the one to whom you pray? You pray to the Creator God of all, the Lord of the universe. He always has existed, reigned, and ruled, and He always will.

You can also remind yourself of God's promises. Like the psalmist did in Psalm 25, remind yourself that you trust in God. Remember that no one who hopes in Him will ever be put to shame.

As you remember who God is and what He's promised, you'll have a better idea of what a privilege it is to pray to Him.

IN YOU, LORD MY GOD, I PUT MY TRUST. I PRAISE YOU FOR WHO YOU ARE. AND I THANK YOU FOR ALL YOU'VE PROMISED AND WILL DO.

BLESSINGS

"Arise, bless the LORD your God forever and ever!
May Your glorious name be blessed and exalted above
all blessing and praise! You alone are the LORD. You have
made the heavens, the heaven of heavens with all their
lights, the earth and everything that is on it, the seas
and everything that is in them. You give life to all of
them, and the heavenly lights bow down before You.
NEHEMIAH 9:5–6 NASB

In the Old Testament, the Israelites returned to Jerusalem and rebuilt the wall. It was a long, grueling, and important process, but once it was finished, they worshipped the Lord for days. Their worship celebration included reading the Law, feasting with joy and praise, and confessing their sins with repentance and fasting. Through it all, they prayed to the Lord. At the center of their prayers was remembering who God is and remembering all of His blessings.

Today, take some time to bless and praise the Lord for who He is and what He's done.

MAY YOUR GLORIOUS NAME BE BLESSED AND EXALTED ABOVE
ALL BLESSING AND PRAISE! YOU ALONE ARE THE LORD.

GO, WORSHIP HIM

Lord, hear me when I call; have mercy and answer me.
My heart said of you, "Go, worship him." So I come to
worship you, Lord. Do not turn away from me. Do not
turn your servant away in anger; you have helped me.
Do not push me away or leave me alone, God, my Savior.

PSALM 27:7–9 NCV

You were created by God and created in His image. It's no wonder you have a longing for Him deep down in your soul. King David's heart told him to go and worship God. If you paid attention to your heart, it also would let you know you need to worship Him. At first, you may misunderstand the calling. You might think other things can satisfy your soul's longing. But God's the only one who will fulfill.

In your prayer time, call on your Father. Ask Him to have mercy and answer you. Also make sure you go and worship Him. Your soul will thank you!

LORD, THANK YOU FOR FULFILLING MY SOUL'S DEEP LONGING!

FORGIVE MY FOOLISHNESS

Then David said to God, "I have sinned greatly by
what I have done! Now, I beg you to forgive me,
your servant, because I have been very foolish."
1 Chronicles 21:8 ncv

Everyone makes foolish decisions. Everyone. Sometimes your foolish decisions end up being silly mistakes, but other times your choices end up being very sinful. When you know you've sinned, you need to deal with it. In fact, the quicker you deal with the Lord over your sin the better.

First, you need to confess you've sinned. Know your error. Admit to it. Once you've done that, turn away from that sin. As tempting as sin may be, or as good as sin might make you feel in the moment, choose to not do it again. Once you've admitted and repented, ask God for forgiveness. King David actually begged God to forgive him.

Admit, repent, and ask for forgiveness—then stay away from making that foolish choice again.

FATHER GOD, I HAVE SINNED GREATLY BY WHAT I
HAVE DONE. I'M SORRY. I DON'T WANT TO DO IT
AGAIN. WILL YOU PLEASE FORGIVE ME?

TRUST IN YOUR LOVE

Lord, look at me. Answer me, my God; tell me, or I will die. Otherwise my enemy will say, "I have won!" Those against me will rejoice that I've been defeated. I trust in your love. My heart is happy because you saved me.

Psalm 13:3–5 NCV

When you face an enemy, it can feel like you're up against the world. Whether you couldn't avoid the conflict or are completely surprised by opposition, it's easy to feel alone.

No one enjoys disagreements or controversy. It can make you feel awful to know that someone opposes you and acts like your enemy. So, what can you do when it happens to you?

For starters, you can pray. Tell God all the painful details and talk to Him about how you feel. Move on to asking Him for help. He can guide you through this conflict. Finally, trust Him and His love. When you call on Him, He can rescue you.

LORD. I TRUST IN YOUR LOVE. I KNOW YOU CAN SAVE
ME FROM ANYTHING AND EVERYTHING!

GLORY

After Jesus said these things, he looked toward heaven and prayed, "Father, the time has come. Give glory to your Son so that the Son can give glory to you."
JOHN 17:1 NCV

Giving glory to something simply means to give honor or praise. Every day you have a choice with what you can glorify. Do you try to seek glory for yourself? Do you put yourself in the highest position and shine the light on yourself? Do you try to glorify something else? Do you ever consider bringing glory to God?

Before He faced His death, Jesus prayed that His Father would give Him glory. But why? Jesus asked for glory so that in turn He could give glory to His Father.

Like Jesus, you can pray that whenever you're in the spotlight, you would bring glory to your heavenly Father. Pray that what you say and do will bring glory to Him, and then when you have the opportunity, make sure you're giving Him all the glory.

FATHER, I WANT TO GIVE GLORY TO YOU IN ALL I SAY AND DO!

A GOOD EXAMPLE

LORD, I trust in you; let me never be disgraced. Save me because you do what is right. Listen to me and save me quickly. Be my rock of protection, a strong city to save me. You are my rock and my protection. For the good of your name, lead me and guide me. Set me free from the trap they set for me, because you are my protection.

PSALM 31:1–4 NCV

Throughout his life, David prayed to the Lord a lot. Fortunately, many of his prayers were written down and shared in the book of Psalms. Because David was very open with his feelings in his prayers, he gave fantastic examples of how you can pray.

Like David, you can tell God how much you trust Him. You can ask Him to save and protect you, both physically and emotionally. And you can ask Him to lead and guide you. Why not try right now?

LORD. I TRUST IN YOU. BECAUSE YOU DO WHAT IS RIGHT. LISTEN TO ME AND SAVE ME QUICKLY. YOU ARE MY ROCK AND MY PROTECTION. FOR THE GOOD OF YOUR NAME. LEAD AND GUIDE ME.

PLEASE GO WITH ME

Then Moses quickly bowed to the ground and worshiped.
He said, "Lord, if you are pleased with me, please go with
us. I know that these are stubborn people, but forgive
our evil and our sin. Take us as your own people."
EXODUS 34:8–9 NCV

Moses was a man who witnessed the amazing power of God. Through miracle after miracle, God worked mightily for Moses and the Israelites. And when it came time for Moses to pray to the Lord, he bowed to the ground, worshipped, and asked the Lord to go with the Israelites and take them as His own people.

In much the same way, before you head off to a new adventure, seek the Lord in prayer. Bow before Him and worship Him. Ask Him to go with you if He's pleased with you. Ask Him for forgiveness. And ask Him to take you as His own daughter.

LORD, IF YOU ARE PLEASED WITH ME, PLEASE GO WITH
ME. I KNOW I AM STUBBORN, BUT FORGIVE MY EVIL
AND MY SIN. TAKE ME AS YOUR OWN DAUGHTER.

FORGIVENESS

If you, L<small>ORD</small>, kept a record of sins, Lord, who
could stand? But with you there is forgiveness,
so that we can, with reverence, serve you.

P<small>SALM</small> 130:3–4 <small>NIV</small>

Absolutely everyone sins. And whether you notice all the ways you disobey God or not, you sin every single day. God is perfect, and He knows all your imperfections. But Jesus can and will forgive your sins. Your belief that Jesus is the Son of God and your choice to let Him be Lord of your life brings undeserved favor with God. Through faith in Jesus, there's forgiveness. Through Jesus, God doesn't keep a record of your sins.

If you've chosen Jesus, the Son of God, to be your Lord, if you've chosen Him to save you from your sins, you're forgiven. You can now live your life with gratitude and service to Him.

JESUS, WITH YOU THERE IS FORGIVENESS OF SINS. WITH YOU
AS MY LORD, I AM FREE TO WORSHIP AND SERVE YOU.

EVERYTHING!

*Lord, you are great and powerful. You have glory,
victory, and honor. Everything in heaven and on
earth belongs to you. The kingdom belongs to
you, Lord; you are the ruler over everything.*

1 Chronicles 29:11 NCV

It can be really easy to fall into the trap of thinking that everything revolves around you. Me, me, me. . .all too quickly you can feel like you're the center of the universe. But the reality? While you are completely unique and no one else has ever been or will ever be like you, you are a human made in the image of God. Like every other human, you have a beginning and ending.

Everything actually revolves around God, though. He is great and powerful. Everything in heaven and on earth belongs to Him. He has no beginning and no end, and He is the ruler over everything. He has glory, victory, and honor. Your prayers are a fantastic place to praise Him for those truths!

LORD, YOU ARE GREAT AND POWERFUL. YOU HAVE GLORY,
VICTORY, AND HONOR. EVERYTHING IN HEAVEN AND ON EARTH
BELONGS TO YOU. YOU ARE THE RULER OVER EVERYTHING.

MY LIFE IS IN YOUR HANDS

Lord, I trust you. I have said, "You are my God."
My life is in your hands. Save me from my enemies
and from those who are chasing me.
PSALM 31:14–15 NCV

It can feel so very freeing to admit that your life is out of your control. But instead of spiraling into absolute chaos, you can rest in the truth that your life actually is in God's hands. He has a plan. Everything is under His control. You can take a deep breath and relax, because it's okay.

As you trust Him as the one who helps and guides you, tell Him in your prayers. He knows your heart, so He already knows you're trusting Him, but telling Him can add a lot of peace to your life.

LORD. YOU ARE MY GOD. MY LIFE IS IN YOUR HANDS.
PLEASE HELP ME RELEASE ALL ILLUSIONS OF
CONTROL AND TRUST YOU COMPLETELY. THANK YOU
THAT WITH YOU I HAVE NOTHING TO FEAR!

GOD IS AT WORK

"We give thanks to you, Lord God Almighty, the One who is and who was, because you have taken your great power and have begun to reign. The nations were angry, and your wrath has come. The time has come for judging the dead, and for rewarding your servants the prophets and your people who revere your name, both great and small—and for destroying those who destroy the earth."
REVELATION 11:17–18 NIV

You can listen to the news and realize very quickly that the Lord is at work. Yes, bad news makes the headlines. And yes, current events seem pretty hopeless. But if you dig in just a little bit and pay attention, you'll be able to spy some of the many ways that God is moving. He moves through people and circumstances. He even works through disasters.

When you notice what He's doing in the world, pray to Him! Recognize His mighty work, thank Him for His protection, and praise His greatness.

I GIVE THANKS TO YOU, LORD GOD ALMIGHTY,
THE ONE WHO IS AND WHO WAS.

WHAT HAVE I DONE?

LORD my God, what have I done? Have my hands done something wrong? Have I done wrong to my friend or stolen without reason from my enemy? If I have, let my enemy chase me and capture me. Let him trample me into the dust and bury me in the ground.
PSALM 7:3–5 NCV

Ever have the feeling that you've done something wrong but you're not exactly sure what it is? You may not be sure why someone seems mad at you. Or you might feel like you're getting an undeserved punishment.

If and when you have those feelings with the Lord, ask Him! Ask Him to reveal if you've done anything wrong and what it is. Then, get ready. You may or may not like what you discover, but you'll know. If you've done something wrong, get ready to confess and turn from your sin. And if you haven't done anything wrong, try drawing closer to the Lord. Get close to Him and learn how to live by following His example.

LORD MY GOD. WHAT HAVE I DONE? HAVE I DONE
SOMETHING WRONG? PLEASE REVEAL IT TO ME!
IF I'M WRONG. I WANT TO CHANGE.

ASK

So the people grumbled at Moses, saying,
"What are we to drink?" Then he cried out to the
LORD, and the LORD showed him a tree; and he threw
it into the waters, and the waters became sweet.
EXODUS 15:24–25 NASB

The Lord showed Himself faithful to Moses and the Israelites time and time again. When they thought they had nothing, He provided. He provided food, drink, and direction.

Even though the Israelites grumbled and complained a lot, you still can learn from their situations and circumstances. You don't have to grumble. When you feel like you have nothing, you can ask the Lord to help you. Ask Him if you're thirsty. Ask Him for energy if you're feeling exhausted. Ask Him to multiply your time if you know you're behind. When you're lacking, ask your Father. He's the giver of good gifts, and He's the God of miracles.

FATHER, PLEASE FILL ME WHEN I'M EMPTY.
WHETHER IT'S A PHYSICAL OR SPIRITUAL NEED, I NEED YOU!

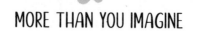

MORE THAN YOU IMAGINE

How precious to me are your thoughts, God!
How vast is the sum of them! Were I to count them,
they would outnumber the grains of sand.
PSALM 139:17–18 NIV

Have you ever stopped to consider the thoughts of God? Really, really pondered them? First of all, it's impossible to imagine all the thoughts He has in just one second, as He holds the entire universe together and knows absolutely everything every single human is thinking and doing. God has so many thoughts, in fact, that there's no way they can be counted. His thoughts are so absolutely precious and beyond anything you can imagine.

Because you can't begin to understand or imagine all of God's thoughts, it's an excellent reason to praise Him. Worship Him for being so much bigger and so far beyond your comprehension. You worship a mighty, magnificent Lord.

GOD, YOUR THOUGHTS ARE SO PRECIOUS TO
ME! HELP ME THINK MORE ABOUT YOU AND LESS
ABOUT MYSELF AND MY CIRCUMSTANCES.

WHAT WOULD YOU LIKE?

That night God appeared to Solomon and said to him,
"Ask for whatever you want me to give you." Solomon
answered, "You have been very kind to my father David,
and you have made me king in his place. . . . Now give me
wisdom and knowledge so I can lead these people in the
right way, because no one can rule them without your help."

2 CHRONICLES 1:7, 8, 10 NCV

One night, God appeared to King Solomon and asked him what he would like. God was willing to give Solomon anything he asked for.

If God asked you the same question tonight, what would you ask for?

Solomon's answer might surprise you. In his choice of just one gift from God, he asked for wisdom and knowledge. Not money. Not power. Not stuff.

Solomon had an important job as king, and ruling the Israelites well meant a lot to him. To rule well, he needed wisdom and knowledge. Just like it was a great request for Solomon, it might be a great request for you too.

FATHER, PLEASE GIVE ME WISDOM AND KNOWLEDGE
SO I CAN LIVE MY LIFE IN A RIGHT WAY.

GOOD TIMES

The LORD lives! Praise be to my Rock! Exalted be God my
Savior! He is the God who avenges me, who subdues
nations under me, who saves me from my enemies.
You exalted me above my foes; from a violent man you
rescued me. Therefore I will praise you, LORD, among
the nations; I will sing the praises of your name.
PSALM 18:46–49 NIV

In a good mood? When you're happy and you know it, your
prayers will surely show it! King David was a man who was
quick to praise God when things were going his way. And
he didn't hesitate to ask God for help when he needed it.

Not only did David thank God for the wonderful ways
He worked, but David also praised God for who he knew
Him to be.

Like David, praise the Lord for who He is when you see
Him working in your life. When you're thrilled, thank Him!

PRAISE BE TO MY ROCK! EXALTED BE GOD MY
SAVIOR! I WILL PRAISE YOUR NAME.

HAVE MERCY

"The tax collector, standing at a distance, would not even look up to heaven. But he beat on his chest because he was so sad. He said, 'God, have mercy on me, a sinner.'"
LUKE 18:13 NCV

Some people are so sure of themselves and so proud of all they've done and what they think they've become. And other people are the exact opposite. Unsure of what they should think or say or do, they're filled with humility. They know they're not the best around and aren't ashamed of that fact, but they accept it to be true.

During Jesus' lifetime, He told a story about a religious leader and a tax collector. The religious leader was very sure of himself. The tax collector wasn't comfortable approaching God in prayer. Instead, he was grieved by his failure, he recognized his sin, and he prayed for mercy.

Jesus then explained how the proud religious leader would be humbled before the Lord. The Lord heard the prayer of the humble tax collector who faced his weaknesses and sin. Who would you rather pray like?

GOD, HAVE MERCY ON ME. I'M A SINNER.

HOW LONG?

How long, Lord? Will you forget me forever? How long will you hide your face from me? How long must I wrestle with my thoughts and day after day have sorrow in my heart? How long will my enemy triumph over me?

PSALM 13:1–2 NIV

When you feel like God isn't answering your prayers, you begin to wonder why. Is He there? Does He hear you? When will He answer you?

Even when you go through times of wanting to know God's response right away, you'll need to wait. Even when you don't see it or feel it, God is working everything out in His own way. And He's working everything out in His own timing.

Since you can't rush God, you'll need to somehow get comfortable with the waiting process. When that seems impossible, tell Him in your prayers. Tell Him how you feel and keep asking Him your requests.

HOW LONG, LORD? HOW LONG WILL YOU HIDE YOUR FACE FROM ME? HOW LONG MUST I WRESTLE WITH MY THOUGHTS? PLEASE ANSWER ME!

LEARNING HOW TO PRAY

Daniel said: "Praise God forever and ever, because he has wisdom and power. He changes the times and seasons of the year. He takes away the power of kings and gives their power to new kings. He gives wisdom to those who are wise and knowledge to those who understand. He makes known secrets that are deep and hidden; he knows what is hidden in darkness, and light is all around him. I thank you and praise you, God of my ancestors, because you have given me wisdom and power."

DANIEL 2:20–23 NCV

Daniel was a man who faithfully tried to obey God. He also was known for his consistent prayers. Taking a peek into Daniel's prayers can be a really helpful way to figure out how to pray.

When it came time to praise God, Daniel did. And he praised Him by telling what he knew to be true about his heavenly Father. You can do the same! Think of all the amazing things you've realized about God and praise Him for it all. Then thank Him for the ways He has answered your prayers.

I PRAISE YOU, GOD, FOREVER AND EVER!

REJOICE!

But rejoice, all who take refuge in You, sing for joy forever!
And may You shelter them, that those who love Your name
may rejoice in You. For You bless the righteous person,
Lord, You surround him with favor as with a shield.
PSALM 5:11–12 NASB

You can learn a lot about the Lord in the prayer of David written in Psalm 5. Like David, you can find your safe place in God. He will shelter you.

The Lord blesses people who choose to live rightly by obeying His commands. In fact, His blessings seem like He surrounds you with His favor like a big, protective shield.

When you feel safe and secure in His shelter and when you recognize His favor in your life, rejoice! Sing for joy! Love your God and His name and rejoice in Him.

LORD. I REJOICE IN YOU! THANK YOU FOR BLESSING ME.
THANK YOU FOR SURROUNDING ME WITH FAVOR JUST
LIKE A SHIELD. THANK YOU FOR YOUR SHELTER.

NOT OF THIS WORLD

*I am not asking You to take them out of the world,
but to keep them away from the evil one. They are
not of the world, just as I am not of the world.*
JOHN 17:15–16 NASB

When Jesus knew His time on earth was coming to an end,
He prayed a very long prayer that included requests for His
disciples and His future followers. If you believe Jesus is the
Son of God and you have asked Him to save and guide you,
that means Jesus was praying for *you*.

What did He pray? He prayed that you would be kept
from the evil one while you're living here in this world. He
also stated a pretty powerful fact: like Jesus, you're not of
this world.

Knowing that you don't have to live like everyone else
in this world is very freeing. When you feel like an outsider
or different from everyone else, it's because you are. You're
with Christ—and with Him is exactly where you belong.

FATHER. THANK YOU FOR CHOOSING ME TO BE
ONE OF YOUR FOLLOWERS. HELP ME REMEMBER
THAT. LIKE JESUS. I'M NOT OF THIS WORLD.

SINCE YOU WERE YOUNG

*God, you have taught me since I was young. To this day I
tell about the miracles you do. Even though I am old and
gray, do not leave me, God. I will tell the children about your
power; I will tell those who live after me about your might.*

PSALM 71:17–18 NCV

If you know the Lord right now, remember that this is only the
beginning of a lifelong (actually, eternity-long) relationship.
And someday, when you're an older woman and you've
known Him and have been praying to Him for decades,
you'll remember the time you spend with Him right now.
You'll remember praying to Him during specific moments
of your life. You'll remember discovering new truths in His
Word. Because you have a forever relationship, start building into it now!

GOD, I AM SO GLAD I WILL KNOW YOU FOREVER. YOU WON'T LEAVE
ME. I WANT TO GET CLOSER AND CLOSER TO YOU EVEN NOW!

RADIANT

*When Moses came down from Mount Sinai with
the two tablets of the covenant law in his hands,
he was not aware that his face was radiant because
he had spoken with the Lord. When Aaron and
all the Israelites saw Moses, his face was radiant,
and they were afraid to come near him.*

EXODUS 34:29–30 NIV

When Moses led the Israelites and would meet alone with the Lord, his face would become radiant. He was so radiant, in fact, that people were afraid to come near him. Spending time talking with the Lord will leave you radiant. You will change on the inside and the outside. You may not scare others, but you'll be noticeably different for the better.

Jesus said His followers would be the light of the world. Spend some time with God to make your light even brighter in this dark world!

FATHER, YOU ARE SO AMAZING! I LOVE THAT BY SPENDING
TIME WITH YOU, YOU'LL CHANGE ME ON BOTH THE
INSIDE AND OUTSIDE. YOU WILL MAKE ME RADIANT.

A SAFE SHELTER

Have mercy on me, my God, have mercy on me,
for in you I take refuge. I will take refuge in the shadow
of your wings until the disaster has passed.
PSALM 57:1 NIV

When the scary storms of life hit, you don't have to try to figure out ways to brave it all on your own. In fact, instead of trying to navigate through your troubled times all by yourself, or even relying on the advice of a friend or family member, find your safety in the Lord. You can run to Him and take refuge, or shelter, in Him. Just like a bird protects its young under its wings, God will keep you safe.

As disaster strikes and you run to God for help, don't forget to cry out to Him for help. Cry out for His mercy. He'll shelter you.

HAVE MERCY ON ME, MY GOD, HAVE MERCY ON ME!
IN YOU I TAKE REFUGE UNTIL THE DISASTER PASSES.

LAST WORDS

Jesus called out with a loud voice,
"Father, into your hands I commit my spirit."
When he had said this, he breathed his last.
LUKE 23:46 NIV

A person's last words are interesting. From funny to wise to loving, the final thing said can reveal a lot about someone's personality. Before He took His very last breath on this earth, the final thing Jesus did was pray to His Father. And it wasn't just any prayer; Jesus put His life in His Father's hands.

Know that as long as you have breath in your lungs, you can pray to your heavenly Father. And know that you can put your life in your heavenly Father's hands at any moment — it doesn't have to be your last one.

FATHER. INTO YOUR HANDS I GIVE YOU MY LIFE.
WHILE I'M STILL BREATHING. PLEASE HELP ME LIVE FOR YOU!

CALL AND ANSWER

I call to you, God, and you answer me. Listen to me now, and hear what I say. Your love is wonderful. By your power you save those who trust you from their enemies.

PSALM 17:6–7 NCV

When you call out to the Lord in prayer, He answers you. He doesn't ignore your call or avoid you. He's never too busy. He wants to hear from you. He listens. And He does all of this out of His wonderful love for you.

Because you can know and trust a kind and loving God who wants a relationship with you, why not talk to Him? Call to Him. Tell Him about your fears and your failures, your dreams and your desires. Open up and share what's on your heart and mind. He will hear absolutely everything you have to say.

I CALL TO YOU, GOD, AND YOU ANSWER ME.
PLEASE LISTEN TO ME NOW. PLEASE HEAR WHAT I SAY.

SHOW

At the time for the evening sacrifice, the prophet Elijah went near the altar. . . . "Prove that you are the God of Israel and that I am your servant. Show these people that you commanded me to do all these things. LORD, answer my prayer so these people will know that you, LORD, are God and that you will change their minds."

1 KINGS 18:36–39 NCV

Elijah knew the one true God. And he needed to prove God's existence to unbelieving people. He did this by challenging false prophets to an epic showdown. (Read 1 Kings 18 for all the amazing details.)

When it came time for Elijah to prove to the unbelieving crowd that the Lord was the true God of Israel, he prayed. His prayer clearly explained who God is. Elijah also asked God to show the people that he was doing what God asked him.

If you find yourself trying to convince unbelievers of the one true God, pray that the Lord would show them and that they would know that the Lord is God.

LORD, ANSWER MY PRAYER SO THE PEOPLE AROUND
ME WILL KNOW THAT YOU, LORD, ARE GOD.

WHAT HE WANTS

*Lord, let me speak so I may praise you. You are
not pleased by sacrifices, or I would give them.
You don't want burnt offerings. The sacrifice God
wants is a broken spirit. God, you will not reject
a heart that is broken and sorry for sin.*

PSALM 51:15–17 NCV

Have you ever thought about what's pleasing to the Lord? Surely you know what pleases you. You know all of your own favorite things and preferences. You probably know what pleases your parents, and you might know what pleases many of your friends. But what pleases God?

Psalm 51 shares what doesn't please God and what does please Him. He's not pleased with sacrifices. He's not pleased with belongings that are offered. What He does want is a person who is sorry about their sin. He's looking for people who are truly upset when they realize they've sinned.

When you pray, ask God to search your heart. And when He reveals sin to you, ask Him for forgiveness!

FATHER, I AM BROKEN AND SORRY FOR MY SIN. PLEASE FORGIVE ME!

MAKER

When the believers heard this, they prayed to God
together, "Lord, you are the One who made the sky,
the earth, the sea, and everything in them."

ACTS 4:24 NCV

Look around you. What parts of the natural world can you see? Can you see the ground? Do you see the sky? How about living creatures or plants? Once you see something natural, think about where it came from. Who was thoughtful and inventive enough to create the dirt and the grass and the trees? Who designed the rivers, lakes, and oceans? Who formed the mountains and deserts?

The Lord is Maker of heaven and earth. He formed all of the natural world. How amazing is that!?

When you consider what He's created, it's time to praise Him! Recognize what He's done and honor Him for it all.

LORD. YOU ARE THE ONE WHO MADE THE SKY. THE EARTH. THE SEA. AND EVERYTHING IN THEM. I AM AMAZED AT YOUR CREATIVITY AND PERFECT PLANS. I AM HUMBLED BY YOUR POWER AND MIGHT!

ACCEPTABLE

May the words of my mouth and the meditation of my heart
be acceptable in Your sight, LORD, my rock and my Redeemer.
PSALM 19:14 NASB

Do you have the habit of dwelling on specific topics or thoughts? Do you often replay the words you said, wishing you would've said something different?

David used a lot of words and considered a lot of thoughts too. And he knew that words and fixations can lead you in a wrong direction. His solution? He prayed that his words would be acceptable to the Lord. He wanted to meditate or consider acceptable topics too.

Like David, it's easy to remember to ask God that your words and your heart's meditations all might be acceptable in His sight.

LORD, YOU ARE MY ROCK AND REDEEMER. PLEASE LET
THE WORDS OF MY MOUTH AND THE MEDITATION OF
MY HEART BE ACCEPTABLE IN YOUR SIGHT.

WHAT HE'S DONE

Both riches and honor come from You, and You rule over all, and in Your hand is power and might; and it lies in Your hand to make great and to strengthen everyone. Now therefore, our God, we thank You, and praise Your glorious name.

1 CHRONICLES 29:12–13 NASB

Time and time again, the Israelites watched the Lord do amazing things. They knew how amazingly wonderful He was and how faithfully He cared for and protected them. So when it came time to pray to Him, they were happy to remember and retell all that He had done.

They knew riches and honor come from the Lord. They knew He ruled over all with power and might. They knew He strengthens people. And they thanked and praised Him.

Like the Israelites, remember how the Lord has worked in your life. Remind yourself of all He's done, and praise and thank Him for it.

BOTH RICHES AND HONOR COME FROM YOU, LORD. YOU ARE POWERFUL AND MIGHTY. AND YOU CAN STRENGTHEN ANYONE. MY GOD, I THANK YOU AND PRAISE YOUR GLORIOUS NAME.

SAVE ME!

Save me, O God, for the waters have come up to my neck. I sink in the miry depths, where there is no foothold. I have come into the deep waters; the floods engulf me. I am worn out calling for help; my throat is parched. My eyes fail, looking for my God.

PSALM 69:1–3 NIV

Some days, life seems to roar and rage and crash over you like a huge wave. Surprised or overwhelmed by what you have to face, you end up feeling like you might drown in the troubles of this world. You feel like you're sinking and can't find a steady place to land.

In those moments of discouragement and despair, cry out for help. Ask God to save you. Beg Him for a divine rescue. Call out to Him for mercy.

Even when you pray, you may not experience immediate relief and rescue. Life might seem unbearable for a while. But keep asking, begging, and calling. Cry out to Him and trust that He will make a way. Because He loves and cares for you, He will save you.

SAVE ME, O GOD! I TRUST IN YOU!

WHY?

Lord, when I bring my case to you, you are always right. But I want to ask you about the justice you give. Why are evil people successful? Why do dishonest people have such easy lives? You have put the evil people here like plants with strong roots. They grow and produce fruit. With their mouths they speak well of you, but their hearts are really far away from you.
JEREMIAH 12:1–2 NCV

When you see the Lord work in your life in wonderful ways, it can be confusing and frustrating to watch evil people prosper at the same time. Why do things go well for them? Why does it look like they succeed? Why do they seem to have things easy?

Instead of focusing on the way other people seem to have easy lives, filled with blessings, try to focus on the blessings God gives you. Since you have enough to be concerned about in your own life, don't fill your time and thoughts with judging others. Keep your focus on God.

LORD, PLEASE HELP ME NOT FOCUS ON WHAT YOU DO AND DON'T DO FOR OTHER PEOPLE. I WANT TO FOCUS ON YOU!

WHAT IS FAIR?

*Lord, hear me begging for fairness; listen to
my cry for help. Pay attention to my prayer,
because I speak the truth. You will judge that
I am right; your eyes can see what is true.*
PSALM 17:1–2 NCV

When life doesn't seem fair, it's because life is *not* fair.
Unfair, dishonest circumstances that shouldn't be allowed
to happen sometimes do happen.

It can be easy to focus on the bad things that happen
to good people and the good things that happen to bad
people. The reality, though, is that bad things happen to
bad people too. And good things happen to good people.

Whether your life seems fair or unfair right now, don't
forget to keep asking the Lord for help. He knows what's
right and true. He will help you out of the trials in your life.
He will bring rest, relief, and rescue.

LORD. HEAR ME BEGGING FOR FAIRNESS.
PLEASE STEP IN AND HELP ME!

WHO AM I?

"But who am I and who are my people that we should be able to offer as generously as this? For all things come from You, and from Your hand we have given to You."
1 CHRONICLES 29:14 NASB

When God knocks your socks off with an amazing blessing, you might find yourself feeling so incredibly grateful but also unworthy. Who are you to receive such an amazing gift from the maker of heaven and earth? After all, God is the giver of all good gifts. All things come from Him. When you see Him at work or when He heaps upon you blessing after blessing, it can make you feel pretty humbled.

Take those moments when your heart is bursting with gratitude and humility and thank the Lord. Remember that all the good things are sweet gifts from Him!

FATHER, THANK YOU! WHO AM I THAT YOU
SHOULD GIVE ME SUCH GOOD GIFTS?

A LIFE OF CONTENTMENT

I will be content as if I had eaten the best foods. My lips will sing, and my mouth will praise you. I remember you while I'm lying in bed; I think about you through the night. You are my help. Because of your protection, I sing. I stay close to you; you support me with your right hand.

PSALM 63:5–8 NCV

No matter what scary or dangerous situations King David faced, he knew God filled his life with good things. He also knew it was good to think about the good gifts from God and to praise Him.

Like David, the Lord is your help. He protects you. He supports you when you're feeling weak. You can stay close to Him and live a life of contentment.

God is a good, good Father. And He generously gives you good, good gifts. When you think about all the good that He adds to your life, make sure to thank Him! In fact, sing to Him. Praise Him when you're thinking about Him.

FATHER, I PRAISE YOU! YOU ARE MY HELP.
BECAUSE OF YOUR PROTECTION, I CAN SING FOR JOY.

HEAR, SEE, AND SAVE

*[Hezekiah] prayed to the L*ORD*: "L*ORD*, God of Israel, . . . You*
*made the heavens and the earth. Hear, L*ORD*, and listen.*
*Open your eyes, L*ORD*, and see. . . . Now, L*ORD *our God,*
save us from the king's power so that all the kingdoms of
*the earth will know that you, L*ORD*, are the only God."*
2 KINGS 19:15–16, 19 NCV

Hezekiah was a king, and he found out the king of Assyria
was ridiculing God. The thing was, the Assyrians were known
to terrorize and destroy other countries. Hezekiah had every
right to be nervous.

Instead of living in fear, though, Hezekiah chose to pray
to God. He asked God to hear and listen, open His eyes, and
see. He wanted all nations to know that God is the only God.

Like Hezekiah, when you have every right to be afraid
or nervous, pray for the Lord to work in a mighty way so
that everyone watching your situation will know that God
is the only God. He's the one who can help you.

HEAR, LORD, AND LISTEN. OPEN YOUR EYES, LORD,
AND SEE. SAVE ME SO THAT EVERYONE WILL KNOW
THAT YOU, LORD, ARE THE ONLY GOD.

HELP ME!

But you, Sovereign Lord, help me for your name's sake;
out of the goodness of your love, deliver me. For I am
poor and needy, and my heart is wounded within me.
PSALM 109:21–22 NIV

Life is filled with highs and lows, ups and downs. Like riding a roller coaster blindfolded, you're never quite sure what's coming next.

Some of life's lows come with conflicts and hurt brought by people. Whether they mean well or are just plain mean, dealing with other people includes getting your feelings hurt. Just as much as you can feel happiness and love, you also can feel sorrow and pain.

When you feel like your roller coaster of life has thrown you for a loop and you're feeling crushed by what someone else said or did, tell the Lord. Pray to Him and ask for His help. He'll give you help, and He'll heal your wounds.

LORD, PLEASE HELP ME FOR THE SAKE OF YOUR NAME!
OUT OF THE GOODNESS OF YOUR AMAZING, LIMITLESS
LOVE, PLEASE DELIVER ME FROM ALL THIS PAIN.

SUPREME!

*God, you are supreme above the skies. Let your glory
be over all the earth. Answer us and save us by your
power so the people you love will be rescued.*
PSALM 108:5–6 NCV

God is supreme. That means He's the greatest in power
and the highest authority in rank in the entire universe.
Nothing is greater than Him. He's supreme in power and
deserves all glory.

When you're in the middle of living your everyday kind
of life, it can be easy to forget His supremacy. It can be easy
to focus on yourself. But your forgetfulness doesn't mean
He's not supreme. He is.

The good news is that anytime is the right time to honor
and praise God for who He is. So tell Him! Tell Him He is
supreme above the skies. Tell Him He saves in an amazing
way and that He alone can rescue the people He loves.

GOD, YOU ARE SUPREME ABOVE THE SKIES.
LET YOUR GLORY BE OVER ALL THE EARTH!
PLEASE ANSWER ME AND SAVE ME BY YOUR POWER.

A HUMBLE PLEA

Then I proclaimed a fast there at the river of Ahava, to humble ourselves before our God, to seek from Him a safe journey for us, our little ones, and all our possessions. . . . So we fasted and sought our God concerning this matter, and He listened to our pleading.

EZRA 8:21, 23 NASB

When Ezra brought the Israelites back to Jerusalem, they faced a long, difficult journey. Instead of hitting the road and fearing all that could come their way, Ezra and the Israelites stopped first to fast and pray. By giving up food and focusing on pleading with the Lord, the Israelites humbled themselves. Not only did they seek God for a safe journey for their lives, but they asked for God to keep their possessions safe too. God listened to their pleading and protected them.

When you face the unknown and are nervous or scared, stop and pray! Plead with God and make your request. Perhaps He will listen to your pleading and protect you, just like He did with the Israelites.

LORD, I PRAY FOR SAFETY FOR ME AND MY POSSESSIONS. PLEASE GUIDE ME AND LISTEN TO MY PLEADING!

THE APPLE OF HIS EYE

Keep me as the apple of the eye; hide me in the shadow
of Your wings from the wicked who deal violently
with me, my deadly enemies who surround me.
PSALM 17:8–9 NASB

When you're the apple of someone's eye, you are the most precious, most cherished person above all others.

You may know who the apple of your eye is, but did you know that you are the apple of God's eye? Your heavenly Father loves you so much! He adores you and protects you. He wants to keep you safe.

As David shares in Psalm 17, not only does God love His children like they are the apples of His eye, but He also will hide His beloved in the shadow of His wings. He protects those He loves from evil enemies.

As you pray, remember you're praying to God who loves you so very much.

FATHER, PLEASE KEEP ME AS THE APPLE OF YOUR EYE!
PLEASE HIDE ME IN THE SHADOW OF YOUR WINGS
AND PROTECT ME WITH YOUR GREAT LOVE.

LET US REJOICE!

Then I heard what sounded like a great multitude,
like the roar of rushing waters and like loud peals of thunder,
shouting: "Hallelujah! For our Lord God Almighty reigns.
Let us rejoice and be glad and give him glory!"
REVELATION 19:6–7 NIV

During your life on earth, if you believe in your heart that
Jesus is Lord, say it out loud, and let your belief shape the
way you live, you'll spend forever worshipping Him in heaven.

What will that worship be like? The book of Revelation
gives glimpses into that worship, including what will be said.
A multitude will praise and give the Lord Almighty glory.

You can practice praising Him with songs that you sing
and prayers you pray. Your lone voice may not sound anything like the roar of a multitude, but God hears and appre-
ciates every word you say. Why not start practicing now?

HALLELUJAH! THE LORD GOD ALMIGHTY REIGNS.
I REJOICE AND AM GLAD AND GIVE YOU GLORY!

HELP ME UNDERSTAND

Help me understand, so I can keep your teachings,
obeying them with all my heart. Lead me in the path
of your commands, because that makes me happy.
PSALM 119:34–35 NCV

Having a good understanding of things is important so that you have a clear idea of what is actually true. Looks can be deceiving, and often matters aren't as simple as they seem. Just like an onion has many layers that need to be peeled away to get to the center, so do certain things in life.

When you want to understand but simply don't, ask God for help. Just like you can ask Him for wisdom in a situation, you also can ask Him to peel back the layers so you get a better understanding. When you do understand a situation better, you can do a great job honoring the Lord with the things you say and do. By asking the Lord to lead you and help you understand, you'll be wiser than many people in this world.

LORD, PLEASE HELP ME UNDERSTAND. AND LEAD ME ON THE
RIGHT PATH TOO. I WANT TO OBEY YOUR COMMANDS!

WHAT TO REMEMBER

*Lord, remember your mercy and love that you have
shown since long ago. Do not remember the sins and
wrong things I did when I was young. But remember
to love me always because you are good, Lord.*
PSALM 25:6–7 NCV

You can probably think of plenty of moments in your life
that you want to remember. And you can probably think of
plenty of moments you wish you could forget. Just like you
feel that way, so did David. But he wasn't concerned about
trying to remember or forget certain things. He wanted God
to always remember His mercy and love. And he wanted
God to forget his sins and all the wrong things he had done.

Like David, you can ask God to forgive and forget your
sins. And you also can ask God to remember to always love
you and show you mercy. He can and He will, because He's
a good, good Father.

LORD, REMEMBER YOUR MERCY AND LOVE ALWAYS BECAUSE
YOU ARE GOOD. AND PLEASE FORGET MY SINS!

REMEMBERING WHO YOU ARE

*Then King David went in and sat before the LORD,
and he said: "Who am I, LORD God, and what is my
family, that you have brought me this far?"*
1 CHRONICLES 17:16 NIV

Have you ever considered who you are? If all of your friends and family were taken from you, if you didn't own any possessions, who would you be? You're just a girl. You're a unique girl who was wonderfully made, but nothing makes you infinitely better than any other girl. After all, people are just people.

You were created in God's image like every other girl, boy, woman, and man on the planet. Yet God still loves you with an unbelievable, incredible love. And He does amazing things in your favor.

That's a lot like King David felt when he asked God exactly who he was to deserve the Lord's favor. David remembered his humble beginnings and knew he was just a man. As much as you and King David are ordinary people, you're also both known and loved by an extraordinary God.

WHO AM I, LORD GOD, AND WHAT IS MY FAMILY,
THAT YOU HAVE BROUGHT ME THIS FAR?

SHOW-AND-TELL

Lord, tell me your ways. Show me how to live.
Guide me in your truth, and teach me, my
God, my Savior. I trust you all day long.
PSALM 25:4–5 NCV

When you were in elementary school, did you enjoy being the center of attention in your classroom or a group of friends during show-and-tell? You got to pick anything to show a crowd of people and then tell them all about what you'd brought.

Much like your classmates and friends needed your explanation to better understand what you were sharing, sometimes you need the Lord to show and tell what He's doing or how He's asking you to live. Humbly ask Him to guide you in His truth and teach you His ways.

As you ask, the Lord will quietly work in your heart and life and begin to show and tell you more of what you need to know. He will guide you and teach you, as long as you follow Him and His truth.

LORD, TELL ME YOUR WAYS! SHOW ME HOW TO LIVE. GUIDE ME
IN YOUR TRUTH AND TEACH ME, MY SAVIOR. I TRUST YOU!

PROMISES

God, I must keep my promises to you. I will give you my
offerings to thank you, because you have saved me
from death. You have kept me from being defeated.
So I will walk with God in light among the living.
PSALM 56:12–13 NCV

A promise is only as good as the person who makes it. In other words, it's important to keep your promises. Avoid breaking them. While this might seem extreme, perhaps the bigger lesson is to be careful what you promise. Only make a promise when you're certain you can keep it. This is true for promises you make among people and promises you make to the Lord.

King David knew this, and he followed up on his promises, whether it was to thank God or to walk with Him throughout life.

Like David, you can thoughtfully make promises to the Lord you intend to keep. Then be sure to follow up and be a promise keeper!

GOD, I WANT TO KEEP MY PROMISES TO YOU. I MUST KEEP THEM!
I PRAISE YOU FOR BEING THE ULTIMATE PROMISE KEEPER.

TURNING AWAY

*But every person and animal should be covered with rough
cloth, and people should cry loudly to God. Everyone
must turn away from evil living and stop doing harm all
the time. Who knows? Maybe God will change his mind.*
JONAH 3:8–9 NCV

After Jonah journeyed to Nineveh to warn the Ninevites
about doom and judgment that would soon come from
the Lord, all the people repented. Once the king of Nineveh
heard the message, he also repented and tried to lead his
people out of destruction.

The king's command? Everyone needed to repent with
outward reminders and inward change. He asked them to
wear sackcloth, a really uncomfortably rough cloth, to help
them mourn. He asked them to cry loudly about their sin.
And he asked the Ninevites to stop doing evil.

The people listened, prayed, cried, and repented in
their sackcloth, and they turned from their evil ways. God
turned from punishing them too. How could your prayers
change events?

FATHER, PLEASE HELP ME TAKE MY SIN SERIOUSLY.
I DON'T WANT TO STRAY FROM YOU AND YOUR WAY!

ONLY A BREATH

"Lord, tell me when the end will come and how long I will live. Let me know how long I have. You have given me only a short life; my lifetime is like nothing to you. Everyone's life is only a breath. People are like shadows moving about. All their work is for nothing; they collect things but don't know who will get them."

PSALM 39:4–6 NCV

Life is quick. Time goes by much faster than you think it should. Some moments drag on and on, and you wonder if you'll need to wait forever. But other days, weeks, months, and years come and go in a flash.

King David knew everyone's life was quick, like a breath. And all of the work a person does in life? It comes and goes.

Even with the speed of life, you can still pray to find meaning in your days. You can ask God to make the most of your time here on earth. Pray He'll use you for His good work.

LORD, YOU GIVE EVERYONE A SHORT LIFE. PLEASE HELP
MY LIFE MATTER! PLEASE USE ME AND MY GIFTS FOR
YOUR GOOD WORK WHILE I AM STILL LIVING.

TEACH ME!

Lord, teach me what you want me to do, and I will live by your truth. Teach me to respect you completely. Lord, my God, I will praise you with all my heart, and I will honor your name forever. You have great love for me.

PSALM 86:11–13 NCV

Being teachable and willing to learn is a very good trait to develop. After all, you can always learn something new.

Instead of just letting lessons pop into your life, though, ask God to teach you. Like the psalmist, ask the Lord to teach you what He wants you to do. Ask Him to teach you to respect Him completely.

His lessons will be good. They'll be taught out of His great love for you. And His lessons will change your life for the better.

LORD. TEACH ME WHAT YOU WANT ME TO DO! I WANT TO LIVE BY YOUR TRUTH. TEACH ME TO RESPECT YOU COMPLETELY.

JUSTICE

God, your justice reaches to the skies. You have
done great things; God, there is no one like you.
PSALM 71:19 NCV

Justice is such a popular topic because everyone wants
to be treated fairly. And it's right to be right, decent, and
just. But don't forget that the creator of justice is God. He
is the one who judges with complete fairness and equity.
He created what is right. As the psalm explains, the Lord's
justice reaches to the skies.

Just picture how high and vast the sky is. If God's justice
reaches to the skies, it's a great reminder that He is so much
bigger than all of that. There is no one like God. He has done
great things, and no prayer is too small or insignificant for
Him. Praise the Lord, the originator of justice!

THERE IS NO ONE LIKE YOU, GOD. YOU HAVE
DONE GREAT THINGS! YOU ARE GREAT!

WHAT HE WANTS

*After walking a little farther away from them, Jesus fell
to the ground and prayed that, if possible, he would
not have this time of suffering. He prayed, "Abba,
Father! You can do all things. Take away this cup of
suffering. But do what you want, not what I want."*
MARK 14:35–36 NCV

It's so easy to get caught up in making your life all about
yourself. Naturally you have your best interest in mind. You
want what benefits you. If your life can be made better in
some way, you're probably pursuing it.

But Jesus showed us our lives aren't always about ourselves. In fact, throughout your life you'll have plenty of
amazing opportunities to choose to glorify and honor God
instead of yourself.

Jesus didn't want to suffer and die on a cross. He knew
how painful and heartbreaking it would be. Yet after asking
God to take away that trial, He also prayed that He might
do what God the Father wanted. You can ask God the
same thing.

FATHER, YOU CAN DO ALL THINGS. I PRAY THAT YOU
WILL DO WHAT YOU WANT, NOT WHAT I WANT.

HURRY!

Please, Lord, save me. Hurry, Lord, to help me. People are trying to kill me. Shame them and disgrace them. People want to hurt me. Let them run away in disgrace.
PSALM 40:13–14 NCV

When you face something urgent in life, of course you want to hurry things along. How can you rush to fix a broken situation? How can you hurry up to get help as soon as possible?

For David, whose very life was in danger, his prayers for help were real. He pleaded for God's protection. Even in the middle of all the threats and terrible tension, God did protect David. He rescued him and kept him out of harm's way over and over again.

Like David, when you know you're facing trouble or you're in the middle of a dangerous situation, pray for God's help. Ask Him to rescue and save you. Beg Him to deal with people who are threatening you, and then thank Him when He does keep you safe.

PLEASE, LORD, SAVE ME! HURRY, LORD,
TO HELP ME. I NEED YOUR PROTECTION!

PROTECTED

God, hear my cry; listen to my prayer.
I call to you from the ends of the earth
when I am afraid. Carry me away to a high
mountain. You have been my protection,
like a strong tower against my enemies.

PSALM 61:1–3 NCV

Your life might be filled with frightening moments. You may feel so afraid you can't help but cry or feel tempted to panic. In those moments of fear, when you have no idea what to do or how to escape whatever trouble you face, cry out to the Lord. Pray to Him for His protection. Tell Him all about your fears and ask for His help.

Once you've prayed, remind yourself how He's protected you before. Look for the ways He's already answering your prayers, and then keep praying.

GOD, PLEASE LISTEN TO MY PRAYER! HEAR MY CRY.
I'M AFRAID, AND I NEED YOUR HELP. THANK YOU FOR
BEING MY PROTECTION AND MY SAFE PLACE!

MY DEFENDER

God, defend me. Argue my case against those who don't
follow you. Save me from liars and those who do evil.
PSALM 43:1 NCV

People can be ruthless and mean. Picky and particular, some mean people can give you a hard time when you least expect it. Bullies might pick on you at any time for no reason at all.

Unfortunately, there's no escaping the need to deal with a person who has set their mind on holding a grudge against you. But you don't have to face these meanies alone. When you face a problem in a relationship, talk to God about it. Tell Him about your fears and annoyances. Talk to Him about your hurt feelings. Ask Him for His help, to protect you or defend you. Ask Him to argue your case and save you from the mean people in your life.

GOD, PLEASE SAVE ME FROM ALL THE MEAN PEOPLE
IN MY LIFE! DEFEND ME AND ARGUE MY CASE FOR
ME. I'M TRUSTING YOU TO PROTECT ME.

SAFETY AND PROTECTION

"I am coming to you now. But I pray these things while I am still in the world so that these followers can have all of my joy in them. I have given them your teaching. And the world has hated them, because they don't belong to the world, just as I don't belong to the world. I am not asking you to take them out of the world but to keep them safe from the Evil One."

JOHN 17:13–15 NCV

Even though you can't see it with your own eyes, a battle between good and evil rages every day. Jesus knew this very well, and as He prayed for His followers, He prayed specifically for their safety and protection from the Evil One.

While you don't need to live in fear, you certainly can echo Jesus' prayers for yourself. Pray that your heavenly Father will protect you from evil.

FATHER GOD, PLEASE KEEP ME SAFE FROM THE EVIL ONE! I AM SO THANKFUL I CAN RELY ON YOU FOR MY PROTECTION AND SAFETY.

WASH IT AWAY

God, be merciful to me because you are loving. Because you
are always ready to be merciful, wipe out all my wrongs.
Wash away all my guilt and make me clean again.
PSALM 51:1–2 NCV

Think about a time when you've been filthy. Maybe you
got really muddy and grime got caked on your skin and
dirt got smeared under your fingernails. Now think about
what it felt like to wash all that mucky dirt off with soap
and water until you were clean again. You felt noticeably
different, didn't you?

When you sin, all the wrong things you do make your
soul dirty. If sometimes you feel gross inside but you aren't
sure why, it might be the filth of disobedience.

Through Jesus, your soul can be clean again. God will
wash away your guilt and shame. He'll wipe away your
wrongs and leave you feeling fresh, clean, and good as
new. To get that cleaning process started, confess what
you've done wrong, ask forgiveness, and ask Him to make
you clean again.

FATHER, YOU ARE SO LOVING AND GOOD! PLEASE WIPE AWAY ALL MY
WRONGS. WASH AWAY MY GUILT. PLEASE MAKE ME CLEAN AGAIN.

THANK YOU!

*God, we thank you; we thank you because you
are near. We tell about the miracles you do.*

PSALM 75:1 NCV

What has God done for you? How have you watched Him work in your life even today? What are some gifts He's given you today? Do you have breath in your lungs? That's a good gift from Him. Do you have food, shelter, and clothing? All are really good gifts. Have you noticed Him work something out that seemed absolutely impossible for you? That's a miracle! Have you felt loved, or surprised by joy? You can thank your Father for those gifts.

Take some time right now to thank God for however you see Him working in your life. Praise Him for the good ways He protects and provides for you. Thank Him for working miracles and for always being near you.

LORD GOD. YOU ARE NEAR TO ME EVEN RIGHT NOW.
THANK YOU! THANK YOU FOR WORKING MIRACLES IN MY
LIFE AND FOR GIVING ME SO MANY GOOD GIFTS.

READY TO SERVE

"Make them ready for your service through your truth; your teaching is truth. I have sent them into the world, just as you sent me into the world. For their sake, I am making myself ready to serve so that they can be ready for their service of the truth."

JOHN 17:17–19 NCV

When Jesus prayed for His future followers, He prayed for things like protection and unity. But He also prayed that His followers would be ready to serve. Specifically, He prayed His followers would be ready for service in the world.

If you choose to follow Jesus, keep His prayer in mind. As you think about how you could or should spend your time, don't forget to include serving others. Just like Jesus spent His life on earth serving, you can too. But as you prepare to partner with the Lord and serve others, don't forget to pray about it.

FATHER, PLEASE MAKE ME READY FOR YOUR SERVICE. USE ME IN PEOPLE'S LIVES TO POINT THEM TO YOU!

BRING IT BACK

Create in me a pure heart, God, and make my spirit right again. Do not send me away from you or take your Holy Spirit away from me. Give me back the joy of your salvation. Keep me strong by giving me a willing spirit.

PSALM 51:10–12 NCV

When you know you've sinned and are feeling far away from God, it's tempting to try to hide what you've done wrong. It might even seem right to ignore your sin and try to forget you ever did it.

The thing is, you can't run from what you've done wrong. Sin will eat away at all your comfort and your peace of mind.

Instead of trying to avoid the fact that you've sinned, confess it to the Lord. Ask Him for forgiveness, and then ask Him for help. Ask Him to make your spirit right again and to create you a new heart in Him. Pray for the Lord to work in your heart and life and bring back His joy. He will!

CREATE IN ME A PURE HEART, GOD!
PLEASE FORGIVE MY SINS. PLEASE RESTORE THE JOY OF
MY SALVATION. BRING BACK MY PEACE OF MIND!

NO ONE ELSE

Among the gods there is none like you, Lord;
no deeds can compare with yours. All the nations you
have made will come and worship before you, Lord;
they will bring glory to your name. For you are great
and do marvelous deeds; you alone are God.

Psalm 86:8–10 niv

Just like talking is the best way to get to know someone and keep in touch with how they're doing, talking with the Lord is a vital way to connect with Him.

When you're talking to God in prayer, remember good rules of conversations: don't focus on yourself the entire time. Talk to Him, and talk about Him! Tell Him what you love and appreciate and respect about Him. Worship and praise Him for the amazing God He is. Remind yourself of who you're praying to, and life will come into focus. Everything is here to bring glory to His name. He alone is God.

THERE IS NONE LIKE YOU, LORD! NO DEEDS CAN
COMPARE TO YOURS. I WANT TO WORSHIP YOU AND
BRING GLORY TO YOUR NAME. YOU ARE GREAT,
AND YOU DO MARVELOUS DEEDS! YOU ALONE ARE GOD.

SCRIPTURE INDEX

OLD TESTAMENT

ABOUT THE AUTHOR

HILARY BERNSTEIN is a Christ follower, wife, homeschooling mom, author, and women's ministry director who loves encouraging and teaching Christian women through her books and blog, hilarybernstein.com.